HUNGRY FOR HOPE

HUNGRY FOR HOPE

*On the cultural and communicative
dimensions of development in
highland Ecuador*

CARMEN G. HESS

INTERMEDIATE TECHNOLOGY PUBLICATIONS 1997

Intermediate Technology Publications Ltd
103–105 Southampton Row, London WC1B 4HH, UK

© Carmen G. Hess 1997

A CIP catalogue record for this book is available from the
British Library

ISBN 1 85339 403 3

Typeset by Dorwyn Ltd, Rowlands Castle, Hants
Printed in the UK by SRP, Exeter

Contents

Abbreviations		viii
Acknowledgements		ix
Preface		xi

1. A story of dead sheep — 1
Introducing a paradox — 4

2. Anthropology and development — 7
An uneasy relationship — 7
Participatory and indigenous knowledge approaches — 9

3. In the parish of the poor — 13
Living in Zumbahua — 15
Ecology and economy — 18
History of Zumbahua — 19
The community of Michacala — 22
    Labour organization — 24
    Kin — 27
    Agrarian structure — 28
    Livestock economy — 29
Conclusion — 31

4. Views on the environment — 34
A scientific view of nature — 35
    Climate and altitude — 35
    Geography — 37
A Michacalan view of environmental forces — 39
    Evil wind — 41
    Taken-by-the-mountain — 42
    Tingu — 44
    Conditions for a good harvest — 45

5. Veterinary and indigenous models of sheep management — 51
Veterinary views of sheep breeding — 55
    Genetic selection — 55
    Nutrition — 56
    Management practices — 58
    Sheep health — 61
A critical review — 64
An indigenous model of sheep health — 67
    Rainbow — 67
    Bad luck — 69
    Sinister person — 71
    Witchcraft — 72

Principles of the indigenous model 73
    Testing the model: protective witchcraft 76
Conclusion 79

6. Hungry for Hope: on the cultural and communicative dimensions of development 82

The rationality debate 82
Dialogue and change 85
Communicative rationality 87
Getting hungry for hope 91

Notes 93

Glossary 101

Sources 102

References 103

Figures, Maps and Tables

Figure 1.   Land use in Michacala   29
Figure 2.   Ombrothermic diagram of Michacala   36
Figure 3.   Four conditions for communicative action   89

Map 1.   Location of the parish of Zumbahua in Ecuador   14

Table 1.   Average family income in Michacala   19
Table 2.   Average animal holding per household   30
Table 3.   Private and boarded animals in Michacala   31
Table 4.   Nutritional value of forage species   57
Table 5.   Sheep illnesses, treatments and efficiency   63

Abbreviations

AID	Agency for International Development
ANCO	Asociación Nacional de Criadores de Ovinos (National Association of Sheep Breeders)
CONAIE	Confederación de Nacionalidades Indígenas del Ecuador (Federation of Indian Nationalities of Ecuador)
GTZ	Gesellschaft für Technische Zusammenarbeit (German Society for Technical Co-operation)
MAG	Ministerio de Agricultura y Ganadería (Ministry of Agricultural and Animal Production)
MIC	Movimiento Indígena de Cotopaxi (Indigenous Movement of Cotopaxi)
NGO	Non-Governmental Organization
PROFOGAN	Proyecto de Fomento Ganadero, MAG-GTZ (Livestock Improvement Project)
UNOCIZ	Union de Organizaciones Campesinas Indígenas de Zumbahua (Indigenous Peasant Organizations of Zumbahua)

Acknowledgements

IN FEBRUARY 1989, I was hired as a researcher by the development project, PROFOGAN (Proyecto de Fomento Ganadero) to study agropastoral production systems in the Ecuadorian *paramo*. PROFOGAN was a German-Ecuadorian project concerned with promoting animal husbandry and located at the Ministry of Agriculture in Quito. The 30 month study was financed by the German Society of Technical Co-operation (GTZ). A grant from the Ecuadorian foundation CAPACITAR enabled me to add another year of research on indigenous knowledge concerning cropping and animal husbandry in the community of Michacala (Cotopaxi Province). I am deeply grateful to the GTZ and CAPACITAR for financing such challenging interdisciplinary research.

Too many people at the Ministry, PROFOGAN and NGOs like CAAP (Cotopaxi), Swiss Aid (Cotopaxi), Mato Grosso (Zumbahua) and the Indigenous Peasant Union UNOCIZ (Zumbahua) lent me invaluable support to mention individually. Thank you all. In Zumbahua and Michacala I benefited from working closely with the project employees Jaime Llanos, Marco Garzón, Luis Toro and Angel Llamuca.

I would like to acknowledge important comments and suggestions from the anthropologist Erwin Frank who has been a constructive discussant of my work throughout those years. Thanks also go to Ecuadorian anthropologists who made my stay enlightening, such as José Almeida, Segundo Moreno and José Yañez del Pozo, my instructor in Quichua.

The research approach in Zumbahua was inspired by the work of Constance McCorkle on Peruvian agropastoralism a decade before our own. She provided high standards for the study that I hoped to emulate. Unique insights into local culture were provided through an ethnography by Mary Weismantel (1988). I was fortunate to have her review my portrayal of Zumbahuan life, pointing out several shortcomings concerning the argument and references.

Previous to research in Ecuador, I received training as a sociocultural anthropologist at the Department of Anthropology at Harvard University. In August 1992 I returned to write up the dissertation. I received intellectual guidance from David Maybury-Lewis, Pauline Peters, Parker Shipton and Evon Z. Vogt (emeritus). Helpful comments on early drafts of individual chapters were provided by Harvard professors Arthur Kleinman and Byron Good, by fellow graduate students Linda Hunt, Juan Carlos Aguirre, Lindsay French, and Bartholomew Dean and by the professionals William Partridge (World Bank) and Traugott Schöfthaler (UNESCO). Thanks go to all of them.

I wish to express special appreciation to David Brokensha, editor of the Indigenous Knowledge Series at IT Publications, whose careful reading and suggestions were substantial to convert the manuscript into a publishable book. Thanks are due also to the editorial team at IT Publications whose efforts made the text more readable. Any errors of fact and interpretation, however, remain my responsibility.

Last, but not least, my eternal gratitude goes to the inhabitants of the community of Michacala and of the town of Zumbahua who offered generous support, and handed over to me the key to their hearts. Without those stimulating conversations amid my newly won friends, this book would have been impossible. *Therefore: Huiñaipac shuc maqui, shuc shuncu, shuc yuyai cashun. Tucuichaimanta yupaichani.*

ix

Preface

HUNGRY FOR HOPE is dedicated to those who believe that by improving cultural sensitivity, and the ability of developers to communicate, development encounters can be transformed into a powerful catalysing experience for the beneficiaries. The author follows what is now a well established method in Indigenous Knowledge studies; she focuses on one particular domain, in one location – in this case sheep-herding in Ecuador – and provides a detailed description and a penetrating analysis. She considers both indigenous and 'western' beliefs and practices. This book aims to reach a varied readership, including those interested in the rural economy and ethnography of the Andes; development; agricultural knowledge systems; participatory philosophy; and communicative action as a novel social paradigm.

The book deals with indigenous people and the problems that plague agricultural production in the high mountains of Ecuador. Chapter 1, 'A story of dead sheep' examines an anti-parasitic campaign for sheep in Cotopaxi Province from the perspectives of the developers and of the rural beneficiaries. The campaign is a telling example, showing how misunderstanding the role of indigenous culture caused the failure of a well-intended and carefully planned campaign.

Chapter 2 reviews the treatment of non-western cultures in development literature after World War II. Considering anthropology's uneasy feelings toward its involvement in development, the current demand for culture-sensitive, participatory approaches provides unique opportunities for anthropologists and sociologists.

Chapter 3 describes the parish society of Zumbahua and the community of Michacala. This portrait helps to contextualize the ethnography of local agriculture and sheep herding presented in Chapters 4 and 5. These chapters examine formal-scientific and local-indigenous knowledge about cropping and sheep herding in Michacala as distinct interpretations of the same reality.

Chapter 6 examines the conflicting interpretations from different positions in social philosophy and theory. Various paradigms are identified by reviewing the 'rationality debate', and by examining proposals by Paulo Freire and Jürgen Habermas who explore the relation between communication and social change and action. When Indigenous Knowledge Systems and Participatory Rural Appraisal approaches are placed in the context of communicative action theory, they will gain theoretical, political and practical significance; and should improve the cross-cultural co-operation for development.

Although based on a study of one small population in the Andes, this volume has much wider implications, and is a welcome and significant addition to our 'Indigenous Knowledge' series.

David Brokensha
March 1997

1 A story of dead sheep

IT WAS A COLD January morning in 1990, when we were administering an extensive questionnaire to Juan, the head of one of 134 families populating the indigenous community of Michacala. We arrived at the section on sheep husbandry and stood close to the family's corral where 10 emaciated sheep huddled together on the muddy ground. Asked why they owned so few sheep, Juan answered that some had recently died quite suddenly. Pressed further, he explained that several men from the provincial capital, Latacunga, had arrived in the village and had promised to cure his sheep so they would be healthy and multiply in the future. They then vaccinated, that is, injected, the animals and soon after several died.

This was the first, but not the last time, we were to hear about vaccines (Spanish: *vacunas*) as the alleged cause of a dramatic rise in sheep mortality in the village of Michacala where we conducted field research on agro-pastoral production during 30 months between 1989 and 1992 for the development project PROFOGAN.[1]

At first, we paid no attention to Juan's story, as he could remember neither the names of the visitors who had treated the animals, nor the institution to which they had belonged, nor even the kind of remedy which had allegedly been injected into the sheep. We only came to have second thoughts when, during a visit to friends in Latacunga, we found out about a large veterinary campaign. The campaign had taken place some months earlier during which several thousand sheep in the entire province of Cotopaxi had been treated against internal parasites.[2] The campaign had been planned and implemented by an NGO (non-governmental organization). Members of the group told us that local sheep owners showed little interest in the treatment of their animals, but, in the end, relatively high numbers of peasants had participated in the campaign – including several from our study community, Michacala. The person from the NGO went on to explain that no more than a certain number of collaborators had been used in every village to demonstrate the benefit of the anti-parasitic treatments to an observing peasantry.

Once we had verified that Juan and a few other Michacaleños had indeed permitted the injections, we were suddenly confronted with the uncomfortable choice either to believe the villagers who linked the death of some of their sheep to those vaccines, or to believe the NGO representatives who assured us that the injections they had administered could not possibly have killed sheep in any large numbers; though they added the rider that an especially weak sheep might have died in response to the physical stress of the treatment. But, they also explained that if this really had been the case, it had happened not because of the anti-parasitic cure but in spite of it.

In the face of this dilemma, we decided to take a closer look. First, we verified that Juan's family had in fact lost a number of sheep after the people from the NGO had treated their animals. We found out that two sheep had died a few days after the vaccines were given. Three others died weeks later. We then contacted other villagers who had also taken part in the campaign and discovered that they had similar complaints to Juan's. Finally, we concentrated on why these villagers actually believed the vaccines and not something else had killed their sheep. They explained in the Quichua language that it was the vaccines in conjunction with cold that had killed the animals: *'llamacuna vacunapash chiripash huañushcacuna'*.

1

At first, we equated the 'cold' with the cool climate prevailing in this community. Michacala is 3700 metres above sea level and the low temperatures are suffered by animals and humans alike. Only slowly did we come to understand that when Juan mentioned 'cold' as an accompanying cause of the sudden death of his animals, he wasn't referring to the ubiquitous low temperatures hovering around freezing point every night, but to a more symbolic kind of 'cold'.

The idea of a cold imbalance is part of a local illness theory applied to both humans and animals, at the centre of which we find the theory of a thermal equilibrium of humours, known to anthropologists as the 'hot-cold syndrome', or illness concept. There are reports from all Latin American countries about the widespread belief that certain illness symptoms in humans are due to a thermal imbalance.[3] According to Michacalan aetiology, a healthy body is in a temperate state of being, while an imbalance towards either a 'cold' or 'hot' condition generates sickness and eventually death. A 'hot' or 'cold' imbalance is not necessarily equivalent to tangible bodily temperatures, though these may sometimes coincide. For example, fever may be taken for a symptom of a hot imbalance but so can be skin disease, or headache. On the other hand, shivering can be indicative of a cold imbalance, but so is coughing, cramp and wind. Therefore, 'hot' and 'cold' should be considered mainly metaphoric terms.

We will describe another instance of local knowledge concerning hot-cold illnesses that will illustrate how the theory works in practice. Rafael, a villager from Michacala, once told us about an illness that had recently struck his father, nearly killing him. One morning his father woke up with a swollen face that turned unrecognizable during the course of the day. Friends and neighbours suggested that he had probably been bewitched, and that he should be brought to a healer to drive out the evil spell. But Rafael remained unconvinced. Instead, he recalled that his father had consumed liquor, and fried fish with pepper sauce and avocado the day before at the market-place in Zumbahua.

Here, we must explain that according to indigenous knowledge, every food item and indeed, every inedible plant or herb, has a position on a cold-to-cool-to-temperate-to-hot scale. In Michacala, for example, cow's milk, beef, barley rice, pepper sauce, fried fish, avocado, and liquor are foods considered to have 'warming' qualities, while a soup with tiny noodles, mutton, rice, potatoes or raw eggs have a 'cooling' effect if consumed.

Bearing these facts in mind, Rafael diagnosed a heat imbalance and turned to the communal health promoter asking him to give his ailing father an injection. Rafael could not recall what kind of injection was given. However, this is a rather irrelevant issue as all injections are generically considered a cooling medicine in Michacala. Our friend's eyes brightened when he told us that his father was perfectly well again the day after the injection.

This brief excursion into the realm of hot-cold illnesses in humans is justified as it is similarly valid in animals too. For example, if a sheep is flatulent, villagers think cold has penetrated the animal. I remember one of those puzzling moments during fieldwork when a woman friend proudly told me that she had cured her sheep of a swollen belly by applying a spicy pepper sauce (Spanish: *ají*) to its anus. However, according to the indigenous theory, it seems logical that 'hot' pepper sauce can be used to counterbalance and cure a 'cold' illness.

After these elaborations on the hot-cold syndrome, we should be able to understand better why Michacaleños thought that vaccines killed their sheep. According to local conviction, vaccines cool down the thermal condition of animals, whether they are thermally balanced, that is, healthy, or already imbalanced toward the cold or hot side. When linking the vaccines to cold, Juan had therefore actually meant to tell us that the injections had either induced or aggravated a cold imbalance in his sheep. So when a few days and even a couple of weeks after the treatment some of his animals died (of whatever cause), he interpreted this as the consequence of the cold treatment with injections.

Let us pause here for a moment and reflect on the principal goal of the anti-parasitic campaign. The NGO had wished to demonstrate the efficiency of anti-parasitic cures in sheep to an indigenous peasantry that was considered largely unaware of the positive effects. To reach that goal, the NGO seems to have taken more than the usual share of conscientious precautions. The NGO contracted the help of veterinary professionals who administered the injections.

The NGO assured itself of the support of the provincial and regional indigenous peasant organizations, guiding the developers to the villages and serving as translators. Finally, the programme was accompanied by an educational scheme in which the particular working of the anti-parasitic treatment was explained to the collaborating flock owners in their own language, Quichua.

Yet despite all these precautions, taking into account technical, linguistic and political aspects, and contrary to the NGO's own assessment, we argue that this campaign failed to reach its stated goal: namely to demonstrate the curative efficiency of anti-parasitic treatments to the peasants because, in fact, the participants in Michacala neither observed the efficiency nor did they show any inclination to repeat the experience on their own accord. On the contrary, their conviction that injections, given to animals not acutely sick of a hot illness, will threaten their very survival had been reinforced.

So, what went wrong? We suggest that the NGO failed to reach its stated goal because of a specific constellation of factors that were not understood in planning and implementing the campaign. First, the NGO believed the local peasants to be unaware as to why their sheep suffered and how to treat them. Second, they expected the flock owners simply to observe that the injected animals became healthier than the untreated ones and, third, that due to this observation, they would arrive at the conclusion that treatments with anti-parasitic injections do their sheep good. Thus, fourth, they would actively look for and administer them themselves in the near future, serving their own best interests as sheep owners. But this did not happen.

At this point of the argument we suggest that the NGO's principal mistake was not to take into account the peasants' knowledge as determining features of their subjectively experiencing and evaluating the vaccinations. In fact, the NGO had no idea of the very existence of the culturally specific ideas presented above. Moreover, even if they had, they most likely would have considered them to be inconsequential beliefs easily disproved by the visible and tangible results of their campaign.

We may ask why peasants like Juan stick so stubbornly to their beliefs concerning the cooling quality of injections instead of accepting the explanations the NGO technicians had given them concerning the working of an anti-parasitic cure. But in putting the question like that, one has succumbed to an unintentional ethnocentrism. Instead, the real question should be: Why should Juan trust the word of a complete stranger over the time-honoured knowledge about vaccines held by his own society?[4]

We may wonder instead why Juan and numerous other peasants actually allowed the NGO to treat their sheep at all. Juan's answer to this question was that the 'Señor Doctor' had repeatedly assured him that nothing bad could possibly happen to his sheep, and that – quite to the contrary – they would soon be far healthier than those of his neighbours. 'The man,' he said, 'talked so nicely that I finally decided to try my luck.' He now very much regretted this decision as he had lost – in his view – five sheep in the experiment and still suffered at home from the constant nagging of his wife, who had vehemently objected to the vaccines from the start. A second answer is that peasants indeed have many problems with their sheep which far too often die without any effective cure at hand. That is, Juan and his peers know that their own knowledge about animal illnesses is often limited and insufficient. It is bitter experience which ultimately induces indigenous peasants to experiment with developers' proposals despite their doubts and fears. But in the end, the local knowledge was apparently proven correct when some animals died after the treatment and their death was linked to the vaccines as the most probable cause. At that moment, the sweet talk of the NGO experts was no longer able to quell local doubts about what vaccines can really do to animals. In the end, the conclusion that the vaccines had killed some sheep seemed to be fairly obvious to the peasants – good intentions notwithstanding.

Introducing a paradox

The case of the veterinary campaign and the conflict between the interpretation of the NGO and those of the peasants testifies to a much more general dilemma in many development projects: namely the lack of adequate cross-cultural under-standing. In our opinion, these shortcomings help to explain a quite common paradox in development projects, namely the enormous disparity between the explicit demand on the part of the indigenous people for outsiders' advice and assistance on the one hand,[5] and their often rather discouraging unresponsive-ness toward much of the advice and assistance finally offered on the other (Foster, 1965; Long, 1977; Turton, 1988; Claverías, 1990).

Ferguson's (1990) writings about peasants in Lesotho strike a very common note. He reports about extension workers of an animal husbandry project who wished to convince their clients of the great advantage of using improved stock and fodder. Finally they were forced to accept 'with frustration that people listened politely to their arguments, and seemed to agree, but afterward refused to follow the advice they had been given.' (Ferguson, 1990: 185).

Another example was put forward by Foster (1973). It illuminates what is really at stake in many intercultural encounters:

> One day, during my fieldwork in Tzintzuntzan, eight-year-old Roberta Caro came down with mumps, but she refused to stay in bed despite the fact that she was quite ill. I offered to pay her medical expenses if her parents would take her to the doctor in nearby Pátzcuaro, an offer they happily accepted. Then I lectured Roberta on the importance of staying in bed, avoiding other children, and, above all, of doing exactly what the doctor prescribed. Roberta agreed to all of this. To my astonishment, the following day I found Roberta playing with her age-mates in the street.
>
> (1973: 144)

Episodes like these turn out to be extremely confusing to many development practitioners; so much so that they may even change dramatically, from a well-intended humanistic identification with their clients, to a decidedly negative evaluation of their characters and disposition. However, Foster is a trained anthropologist and so continued his search for a better understanding of the situation. He solves the riddle of Roberta's mother's decision-making and describes his discovery in the following words:

> I remonstrated with her mother, who replied, 'But the doctor told Roberta that she should bathe.' Then I understood. In Tzintzuntzan no one bathes who is ill, a taboo that continues until complete recovery. To announce, after an illness, 'I have bathed,' is to declare publicly that the speaker is completely restored to normal health. The doctor presumably thought he was fighting germs by telling Roberta to bathe, to stay clean, but her mother, not surprisingly, in view of the cultural meaning of bathing, interpreted his words to mean, 'Since she can be bathed, now she is well.' Health education and medical treatment had a consequence entirely different from that intended by the doctor.
>
> (1973: 144)

We suggest that lack of understanding, miscommunication and negligent behaviour are related phenomena and quite regular occurrences in development projects around the globe. It does not need much imagination to accept development workers' frustration about the sometimes puzzling results of the interaction with their clients. Their frustration can turn into plain rejection, if it happens that those clients still do not act as they are advised, even though the advantage of what has been advised has been practically demonstrated. In such cases, development practitioners may even feel driven to the conclusion that something must be wrong with their clients' personalities, or even mental capacities.

At the heart of this predicament is that many development practitioners tend to see those they deal with as basically identical to themselves in their way of experiencing a world that is objectively given. This is likely to happen because many change agents ignore the existence and content of indigenous knowledge. Even if some practitioners become exposed to, for them, unusual bits and pieces of knowledge, they discount them. Instead, we argue that such an approach is often bound to fail. Co-operation for development is an intercultural endeavour which demands sound communication across separate knowledge systems to reach mutual agreement on concrete and – for all – rational action.

The observation that cultural and cognitive disagreement is at the root of many project failures is not new. Since the ground-breaking edition on *Indigenous Knowledge Systems and Development* by Brokensha et al. in 1980, indigenous knowledge is considered a basic foundation to local decision-making processes. This contribution has stimulated research on indigenous knowledge systems (IKS) which materialized recently in an augmented and improved edition by Warren et al., *The Cultural Dimension of Development: Indigenous Knowledge Systems* (1995).

Two analytical concepts provided by the IKS scholars have proven particularly helpful for guiding further research: namely the distinction between indigenous patterns of perception (Indigenous Knowledge System), on the one hand, and scientific, or internationalized patterns of cognition (Formal Knowledge System) on the other. Indigenous knowledge is defined as

> local knowledge that is unique to a given culture. It is the information base for a society which facilitates communication and decision-making. Indigenous information systems are dynamic, and are continually influenced by internal creativity and experimentation as well as by contact with external systems.
>
> (Flavier et al., 1995: 479)

The main difference, then, between indigenous and formal knowledge systems can be summarized as follows:

> The formal knowledge system is generated in educational settings such as schools, universities, research institutes and is circulated through the global network of professionals, institutions and specialized publications.
>
> (Warren and McKiernan, 1995: 426ff)

Using the distinction between indigenous and formal knowledge systems, Chapters 4 and 5 will show why a scientifically grounded problem analysis of the agricultural production system in Zumbahua contains a strange set of unconnected propositions for local peasants, which clashes head-on with central themes of their own cognitive system. Our argument is that whenever such clashes occur, the developers' points of view and advice have very little chance of ever being accepted and implemented by their clients. This book attempts to give a fresh perspective on this dilemma and supplies a potential solution.

2 Anthropology and development

IN THE INTRODUCTORY CHAPTER, we examined the cultural dimension of development by evaluating a veterinary campaign. The campaign hoped to demonstrate the effectiveness of an anti-parasitic treatment in sheep to the indigenous peasantry. We found that the effects of the campaign were observed and interpreted quite differently by the peasants than the campaign organisers anticipated. We now move from this particular case to the treatment and conceptualization of culture in development theory as discussed since World War II. Such contextualization allows us to locate our own perspective on the cultural dimension in development into a general theoretical debate. This will enable us to point at the paradigm shifts in dealing with the culture as an analytical category, and to highlight the exciting potential which contemporary development-related social sciences provide for rethinking anthropologists' participation processes of change.

An uneasy relationship

The past relationship between anthropology and development has been highly antagonistic. Development has been strongly criticized as an ethnocentric, morally questionable, politically mystifying and ambiguous concept or metaphor. Among the more radical critiques are those forwarded by Bello et al. (1982), Sachs (1992), Erler (1985), Goulet (1985), Escobar (1991) and Ferguson (1990). With no alternative, the term development, as used in this book, refers to a professional field concerned with planned and controlled social and cultural change. This immediately triggered irritation in anthropologists who were hesitant about changing the way of life of those they studied. This cannot simply be called a professional flaw of anthropologists as such a critical attitude is grounded in the fact that much of so-called development has had disastrous implications for exactly those people anthropologists deal with: ethnic and tribal minorities, poor, and relatively powerless, people.

Another reason for a sceptical attitude of anthropologists towards applied fields like development has been the fear of losing their independent judgement once they work for an employer 'outside the halls of a university' (Clifton, 1970: xvi). Uneasy feelings about engaging in development processes were strongly enhanced during the 1960s by the critique of dependency theory which implied that any attention of the First World towards the Third World must be considered an attempt to safeguard the economic and political hegemony of the industrialized élites over the poverty-stricken remainder of the world in a postcolonial yet still neo-imperialist era. This seemed true enough, as cases of the direct involvement by anthropologists in political interventions with clear military purposes, such as in Vietnam or Chile (Horowitz, 1967), became public. Understandably, such incidences have fostered suspicions among anthropologists, and fuelled a discussion of anthropology's origin in the colonial enterprise and its permissive participation in the whole process of colonial exploitation.[1] The claims that anthropology and anthropologists could protect the interests of the oppressed, abused and poor people they study has become equated with political naïvety in face of the overall structure of a capitalist world system (Wallerstein, 1974) marked by extreme inequality and dependency between the rich and poor countries (Cardoso and Falletto, 1979; Frank, 1967; Amin, 1974).

Unquestionably, the gap between the industrialized centre and its less de-veloped periphery seems more likely to widen than to close. Inequality built into the structure of the relationship between centre and periphery makes it likely that much of the development process in the Third World will only serve the interests of the dominant élites, and even further restrict the possibilities of the 'victims of progress' for building a better future for themselves (Bodley, 1982). Yet, we sympathize with those anthropologists who argue that – for precisely the same reasons – we have a moral obligation to help construct a vision and a world that is more humane and just.[2]

In fact, a growing number of anthropologists assume special responsibility as they are drawn into intimate relations with people who suffer the consequences of an unjust international as well as national order (Hoben, 1984). Although anthropologists seem to have little to offer in terms of economic or political influence, money and power alone are not always all that is needed for fostering authentic change among impoverished groups. There is something very import-ant which anthropologists can offer: namely, their skills as informed intermedi-aries between those who have access to money and political power and those who lack both, but seek improvement of their quality of life.

We now turn to culture and its use as an analytical concept in development circles. Respectively, we rely on several reviews of anthropological involvement in development since World War II (Long, 1977; Worsley, 1984; Eddy and Partridge, 1987; Cochrane, 1979; Bennett, 1988; Robertson, 1984). In the two decades following World War II, the view that people's cultural manners and preferences can be a barrier to their society's modernization became entrenched. This judgement resulted from the disappointing experiences with development assistance to non-western countries, where a success like that in post-war West-ern Europe could not be repeated.

This was the more devastating as, then, the economic prospects for the world's future in general were seen in a highly positive light in economic terms. Modern-ization theory of the 1950s suggested that even very poor nations could, in principle, follow the example of industrialized nations and realize a prosperous future, if only aimed in the right direction (Rostow, 1964; Eisenstadt, 1973). The seriousness of obstacles to modernization, however, had rapidly become appar-ent. One conclusion was that people either prevented modernity from becoming a part of their environment (supposedly because of nostalgia for traditional ways of life), or they prevented established modern structures from functioning ade-quately because of the incompatibilities of their culture with modern life – an argument that still circulates today even if it has become more of a whisper.[3] In any case, cultural barriers to modernity and progress soon came to be identified everywhere as development programmes have been undertaken without success (Foster, 1969, 1973; Cochrane, 1979).

Development-related social theory in the 1960s was still a reflection of this all-embracing expectation about modernization, based essentially on an economic growth model. As Third World countries failed to prosper, this development model came under heavy attack from the Marxist and progressive camps. De-pendency theory became the declared opponent of modernization theory and was put forward to explain the resilience of poverty and inequality in Third World countries. It took a different perspective by explaining the unequal de-velopment of Third World countries with reference to unfair terms of trade between them and the industrial centres, which prevented closure of the econ-omic gap (Frank, 1967). On the contrary, speculation began that the gap was continuously widening; in other words, the rich countries got richer and the poor ones poorer.

This predilection of modernization theory to identify country- and culture-specific traits in order to explain stagnant or recessive development was criticized from the new perspective of dependency theory as an ideological camouflage to cover neo-imperialist, exploitative interests of the industrialized centres and economic élites in Third World countries. Research assigning cultural barriers to social change and development, seen from this perspective, appeared to be mere pseudo-explanations (Robertson, 1984: 49). They were atheoretical, apolitical and ahistorical contributions and hence irrelevant to the debate about the true causes of underdevelopment (Long, 1977: 51–2, 72).

Dependency theorists also concluded that the so-called traditional structures and pre-capitalist modes of production were falsely blamed for constituting obstacles to economic growth whereas, in fact, they served the very interests of the élites in maintaining the unequal status quo as the poor masses provided conveniently cheap labour to the rudimentary industry and export sector of the Third World countries (Harriss, 1982). In essence, culture as an analytical concept in explaining or investigating change processes virtually disappeared in this period.

In the late 1970s culture appeared again on development indexes alongside economic, political, ecological and social variables which were said to influence change processes. Still, culture was usually put at the end of the list, apparently relegated to lesser importance compared to the other factors. However, there had been a change since the 1950s, namely, that culture was seen not only as an obstacle to social change, but as an instrumental means of bringing it. From this, it follows that anthropological expertise has been sought to facilitate the transfer of knowledge and technology to development projects. This approach has again fed the fears of many anthropologists about being used as handmaidens for engineering change processes via the cultural manipulation of the targets of development (Swantz, 1985: 31) and without consideration for the best interests of the people involved. Anthropologists can deal with this concern in more constructive ways since participatory philosophy and indigenous knowledge research are influencing development thinking. The ideas and methods offered by both approaches seem to introduce a positive quality to anthropology's involvement in development.

Participatory and indigenous knowledge approaches

We can count again on a bold acceptance of the cultural dimension of development as most advisers accept that they have to respond to the development problems, needs and goals as their clients themselves define them. But although participation of local people during the planning and implementation phases of their projects has already become a key concept of the development philosophy since the 1980s, we believe that the particular difficulties of achieving authentic participation have been underestimated or incompletely understood.[4]

In the meantime, however, many development-related researchers and practitioners have elaborated valuable ideas about indigenous cognition and tested techniques to improve and enhance local participation in development projects. Among those trends, we wish to highlight two of these ideas. First, Indigenous Knowledge Systems (IKS) Research which has contributed to a better understanding of indigenous knowledge about agriculture and natural resource management. Second, the advances achieved by representatives of PA (Participatory

Appraisals) and their respective tool kits to stimulate genuine local engagement in the change process.

Conditions have changed significantly since Swantz formulated the question that has plagued many anthropologists involved in development practice: 'Can an anthropologist pursue the goals and principles of his/her discipline and at the same time cooperate with development agencies?' (1985: 26–7). The answer from anthropological observers like Escobar (1991) is decidedly 'no' as he reduces development anthropologists to people who are limited to reinforcing ethnocentric, Western models of development, and who put themselves at the service of the powers that be. While, anthropology's involvement in development has not been free of contradictions, yet we can agree with an observation made by Sillitoe (1993) that currently the development community is seriously interested in constructive and practical proposals from an anthropological and sociological perspective. We also argue that development-related social scientists have generated methodological and research devices that offer promising opportunities for getting involved in planned change while continuing to observe the ethical principles of the anthropological discipline.

In general, IKS researchers study the time-honoured knowledge and performances of a specific people towards this-worldly activities in the fields of agriculture, health, family planning, literacy and nutrition which are basic to all cultures and times. Their research methods are multidisciplinary, stemming from the biological, social, humanistic or applied sciences (such as action research, ethnoscience, agro-ecosystem and farming system research and concomitant fieldwork. Local cognition and techniques are usually studied from an emic and an etic point of view, separating insiders' from outsiders' interpretations of the very same fact.

One distinct merit of IKS research is that it successfully counteracts the negative image of indigenous people, farmers and herders as 'irrational', 'ignorant', or 'risk-averse' entrepreneurs. Using scientific methods and generating data and proof acceptable to formally educated natural scientists and technicians, it achieved what all previous philosophical arguments about cultural relativism could not: the recognition of indigenous knowledge and expertise as experimental, economically sound and often more appropriate to the local situation than purely 'scientific' suggestions.

Today, we have begun to criticize that this endeavour to rectify the propriety of local decision-making as rational, knowledgeable and experimental has led to the counter-stereotype of the always-competent peasant (Fairhead, 1993: 187). We are sure, however, that a balanced perspective on the expertise of indigenous people will eventually emerge in the near future, having once overcome the intellectual stalemate of the previously negative stereotype of the incompetent farmer. Taken together, the greatest contribution of IKS research was to generate quality information on local knowledge and practice which can be used to enhance the cultural competence of developers who wish to communicate and co-operate with people from other cultures.

The abbreviation PRA can stand for Participatory Rural Appraisal, Participatory Relaxed Appraisal or Participatory Rapid Appraisal. The main characteristic of all participatory approaches – according to Chambers (1983) and Cernea (1991) – is to put 'people before things' and thus reverse the dominant paradigm of the 1960s to 1970s which prioritized material, infrastructural improvements and economic growth. Participatory approaches seek the influence of development clients on the respective decision-making processes and planning instead of just bringing them in at the implementation of projects (Bhatnagar and Williams,

1992: 177). Ideally, a participatory approach in development planning gives local people ownership over the change process as they have defined it themselves.

Chambers defines PRA as 'a growing family of approaches and methods to enable local people to share, enhance and analyse their knowledge of life and conditions, to plan and to act' (1994b: 1437). Wright and Nelson (1995: 59) rightly point out that PRA reverses the relationship between researcher and researched by making the latter participants and subjects in their own research. In fact, extension agents and researchers change from experts into facilitators of the local problem solving process. Among the more tested appraisal tools are: participatory mapping, transect walks, matrix scoring, well-being grouping, institutional diagramming, seasonal calendars and trend analysis. We would also like to mention *GRAAP* and *Road to Progress* as examples for appraisal methods that are more complex and dialogical than most of the aforementioned PRA tools and excellent for defining and analysing problems with local people.[5]

These and other participatory methods generate quality data, if applied professionally. They allow local people to investigate and analyse their own problems and develop locally appropriate solutions (Chambers, 1991: 527). Participatory methods have raised high hopes among developers and clients because they can fulfil what they promise: true participation of the people. Such success has contributed to reversing the cognitive framing, mode of interaction and power relations between developers and clients. They have put voice, vote and decision-making into local hands (Chambers, 1994a: 1262–6). Those of us who have become acquainted with complex participatory appraisal and planning tools like the *Road to Progress* and who have experienced their action-motivating power are getting hungry for more.

If we then reconsider the comment of Pottier (1993: 11) who maintained that it has become common knowledge that the developer has to 'listen and to learn' but that it still remains unclear how such listening and learning can be achieved; we may counter today that various strands of IKS and participatory research have contributed significantly to the 'how to'. IKS research provides us with systematic insights into indigenous cognition and practice. Participatory approaches help locals to express their ideas, discuss them, define priorities, reach consensus and finally act upon them.

We feel that much progress has been made. Yet much still remains to be done. One shortcoming is that both approaches focus on a kind of intercultural communication which is still one-way in nature: namely from locals-to-developers. This reverses the earlier unhealthy situation in which developers attempted to convince their clients of new ways of producing and living; but truly good communication must always be two-way. It is our contention that IKS and participatory research and techniques can improve.

Similar observations have been made by others. Bebbington (1991) finds it possible to link and move between indigenous and formal knowledge systems. Such lack of interaction between holders of distinct knowledges also underlies a comment by Slikkerveer and Dechering (1995) who write that

Within the development related social sciences and in particular in development anthropology and sociology, few studies of the concept of Indigenous Knowledge Systems have so far tended to focus on the interaction between local structures of perceptions and practices on the one hand, and outside forces of innovation, development and social and cultural change on the other.
(p. 436)

Hungry for Hope

These comments lead up to the principal concern in this book: namely that the greatest challenge to the social sciences is to develop non-ethnocentric theories and tools to facilitate dialogue and legitimate interaction between members of distinct cultures.

3 In the parish of the poor

AFTER A SIX-MONTH STUDY and visits to 27 Ecuadorian high-altitude parishes in 1989, our project, PROFOGAN, decided to work in Zumbahua, a parish of poor peasants (Map 1). We found Zumbahua a suitable research site to study typical agricultural problems in *paramo* zones.[1] Within the parish we selected the community of Michacala to study one particular agropastoral production system in detail.

This chapter will introduce the high mountain society, economy and history of Zumbahua. We will elaborate on the complex exchanges of natural resource use and labour between peasant families, compounds and communities, imposed by the ceaseless human efforts to secure a livelihood under extremely arduous conditions. We emphasize the ingenious ways local people try to overcome their environmental limitations without wishing to deny that all their efforts afford them no more than the most meagre sustenance with which they themselves are far from satisfied and which makes them hope for a brighter future for their children.

Zumbahua is the name of both a small town and a parish belonging to the Province of Cotopaxi. It is connected to the capital of its canton, Pujilí, and to the provincial capital of Latacunga by a gravel road that climbs from 2700 m to the top of the western *cordillera*, reaching an altitude of some 4500 m at its highest point. At this height, one finds vast stretches of yellow-greenish mountain grasslands, where sizeable herds of sheep pasture side by side with llamas, donkeys and pigs. The animals are usually tended by children, young women or elders, accompanied by one or two emaciated dogs. Descending on the now rapidly decaying road to the west, the traveller enters an area where the grasslands have long since given way to fields of potatoes and other Andean tubers such as *oca*, *mashua* and *melloco*, interspersed with fields of beans, barley and shallots. At this point, the traveller has already crossed the watershed separating the inter-Andean valley of Latacunga-Ambato, which drains to the Amazon via the Pastaza River, and the coastal region of Ecuador, entering the upper drainage area of the Toachi River that flows north-west to the Pacific Ocean.

The landscape has a wildly romantic character due to the sharp silhouettes of eroded mountains and the gigantic rocks spread over cultivated plots (Quichua: *chacras*) that cling to steep slopes. The beauty of the landscape cannot blind us to the fact that this is an area whose altitude makes it virtually unfit for agriculture. It is amazing to see a place where even the natural vegetation has a hard time clinging to the slopes, yet people are transforming these same slopes into fields.

Tiny houses are spread out to the left and right of the road, only rarely forming villages. Most of them are still made of adobe with thatched roofs, but some houses are built of concrete blocks with zinc roofs. Usually few people are to be seen. Here and there a woman may lead a donkey or llama home loaded with freshly cut *paramo* grasses, or someone may sit patiently by the side of the road, waiting for a bus. Most probably heading for one of the cities of the inter-Andean valley – Latacunga, Ambato or most likely Quito – hoping to find employment as an unskilled worker. Part of the scene are skinny dogs, barking ferociously and running close to the wheels of the departing vehicle. A Zumbahuan woman explained to us why dogs follow buses so insistently: a long time ago a dog took a ride on a bus and was short changed by the driver; as a result, dogs follow cars because they still try to recover their money.'

13

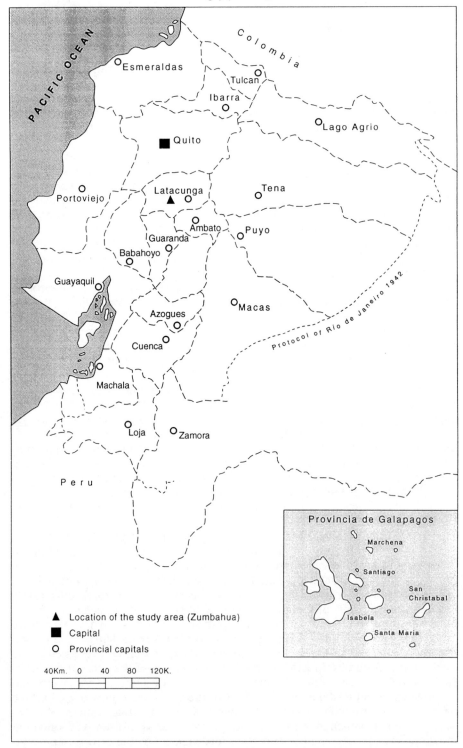

Map 1   *Map of Ecuador showing the location of Zumbahua*

Living in Zumbahua

The parish of Zumbahua divides into a lower and an upper section at an altitude of about 3700 m. Its lowest part, an elongated flat valley bottom, is bisected by the deep gorge of the Zumbahua River (which is nothing but the upper reach of the aforementioned Toachi River). The parish plain is 3500 m above sea-level and is surrounded on all sides by high mountains. In a southern corner of the plain is the parish centre, the tiny town of Zumbahua itself, roughly 65 km from Latacunga or a two-hour bus ride. The town is small, home to only 110 families, totalling some 500 inhabitants. Few white and black families live here among a vast majority of indigenous people, while the absence of so-called *mestizos* is striking (Stutzman, 1981).[2] Generally, these white and black families engage in trade and keep stores in the parish town; they are descendants of ex-employees of what was until 1964, the hacienda of Zumbahua.

The official census of 1982 listed 9000 inhabitants for the parish of Zumbahua (CEDIG, 1985: 14–15), while the most recent census of 1990 listed only 4350 (INEC, 1991). However, this significant decrease in population is suspect, especially since it cannot be attributed to rural–urban emigration. In general, Zumbahueños migrate to the cities only temporarily, in search of wage labour, and do not abandon their villages. Husbands work for a weeks at a time in the urban centres while their wives and children stay at home. What might explain the discrepancy between both counts is that they are only rough estimates be- cause the Zumbahuan people have refused to participate in any census and have never been accurately counted. We made an unofficial estimate that we consider closer to the actual demographic reality of the parish, totalling some 15 000 people. Our estimate was based on interviews with representatives of all *comunas* within the parish. These 9000 to 15 000 Zumbahueños live scattered throughout the total parish territory of 230 km[2], comprising Zumbahua town, and some 10 indigenous *comunidades*: La Cocha, Quilotoa, Chami, Chimbacucho, Huantopolo, our study community Michacala, Talatac, Yanatoro, Yanallpa and Saraucsha.[3]

A notable feature of the town of Zumbahua is the huge Salesian Mission buildings that border the central market-place. The impeccably white-washed mission church is especially eye-catching. The church is surrounded by tidy houses where the Salesian monks and nuns live. Directly connected with the Salesian Mission, and living within the same compound, are some Italian volun- teers belonging to a group called Mato Grosso. They offer religious assistance but spend more time involved in small-scale projects in agriculture, crafts or in infrastructural improvements, and even in the general and professional educa- tion of Zumbahuan youth. They have worked in Zumbahua since the mid-1970s. The Mission, together with the Mato Grosso volunteers, has become central to Zumbahuan life in many ways.

The town of Zumbahua was not connected to the national electricity grid until 1991. It therefore depended entirely on a petrol-generator owned by the mission to provide it with daily electricity between seven and nine at night. Although Zumbahua was finally connected up to the national power lines in 1991, the surrounding communities still lack electricity. The Mato Grosso people again played a crucial part in the planning of the infrastructure and in organizing the local labour force needed for the project. This was similarly the case a decade earlier, when pipes for drinking water were installed in the town. Most of the parish communities, however, still lack these modern services: electricity, drinking-water, garbage disposal or simple closed toilets. The severe toll this neglect engenders became very apparent recently when cholera broke out and spread quickly throughout rural Ecuador, claiming lives particularly in poverty-stricken places like Zumbahua.

The Salesians also run a high school in Zumbahua in direct competition with a state-run school. For years attendance at the latter has been dwindling while its missionary equivalent has been doing exceptionally well. The whole parish in comparison even with other indigenous parishes shows an extremely low stand-ard of primary education. Even though every community in the parish now has its own primary school, attendance is moderate and the drop-out rates are high. This is because children are often needed by their families to do chores. More-over until quite recently schooling was carried out entirely in Spanish, which most pupils entering school were unable to understand or speak.

In fact, the indigenous population of Zumbahua remains monolingual in Quichua, even though their Quichua dialect is embroidered with many Spanish words. Most men obtain a good working knowledge of Spanish as a result of their recent migrations to Quito and other cities in search of jobs. Yet the intra-family and village language in the entire parish remains Quichua. Illiteracy is still the rule. Indeed, at least two-thirds of the adult population of this parish can neither read nor write, either in Spanish or in Quichua (Source 2). Some years earlier, Mato Grosso volunteers mentioned an even higher per centage – of up to 90 per cent illiteracy (Córdoba et al., 1988).

When compared to the mission buildings everything else in Zumbahua appears somewhat shabby and run down, including the two rest houses for tourists, the grocery stores, and the bars (Spanish: *cantinas*) near the market-place. The stores sell a broad assortment of items: noodles and rice, sweet drinks, popular medicine, cooking gas, knitting materials, *tragu* (sugar-cane liquor), and so on. They are open every day but hardly patronized on weekdays. There is also the office of the local state representative (Spanish: *Teniente político*), looking as run down as all the other buildings, but recently extended to house a tiny prison. From there, the highest secular parish authority, namely the *Teniente Político*, adjudicates legal and social quarrels among parish inhabitants, a seemingly fre-quent occurrence, if the large office crowded with complainants during office hours is any indication.

Another building of great importance to the population is the medical post (Spanish: *puesto médico*). No published data exist on the overall health situation within the parish, although we were given casual information by the medical post employees: two medical graduates and three nurses in their first year of medical practice, all doing an obligatory one-year period of service. According to them, the most frequent illnesses among adults in the parish are tuberculosis, ulcers, and gastro-enteric problems. Infant mortality was recorded as 200 out of 1000 live births in 1990. This is three times the national child mortality (WHO, 1992: 52), and double the average for the canton of Pujilí. How bad the health situation really is becomes apparent when one sees the long queue of patients waiting in front of the medical post for treatment every Saturday.

Throughout the week, Zumbahua is a sleepy town indeed. Only on Saturday mornings does it suddenly spring to life, thanks to its market. On Friday eve-nings many *cholo*[4] merchants arrive from towns like Latacunga, Saquisili and Ambato, or from the coastal towns of La Maná and Quevedo. They immedi-ately start to set up stands where they will sell clothes, farm implements, medicines, or staples like rice, noodles, flours and fruits the next morning.

Usually, some local women also put up poles with plastic sheeting to protect their customers from the sometimes rainy, sometimes dusty and always icy winds that plague Zumbahua year in and year out. Here they will sell dishes of chicken, fried fish or soups.[5]

Early on Saturday morning, people from the whole parish pour into town, soon filling up the market-place and the roads leading to it. Those from higher altitudes bring loads of shallots carried by llamas, which they sell either in smaller bunches to the parish inhabitants or in sacks to traders. Those from lower villages bring garlic, potatoes and barley. Some 60 men and women will offer sheep, goats, llamas, donkeys or pigs for sale, immediately using most of their earnings to buy oil, rice, noodles and some bread and fruit for their children back in the village.

However, the quick pace of activity in the market cannot conceal the fact that the nature of the transactions reflects the depressed economy of the parish. What locals normally bring here to sell has taken them months and – in the case of animals – even years to produce, while most of the merchandise they take home, purchased with the money they earned from selling their produce, is relatively expensive and rapidly consumed. In other words, the terms of trade between local products and 'imported' consumer goods such as processed food are extremely unfavourable for the Zumbahuan farmers, which is, of course, one of the main reasons why they remain poor.

For example, a hat, which is – culturally speaking – an absolute necessity for men and women, old and young in Zumbahua, costs as much in cash terms as a regular *paramo* sheep that required three years of daily herding and care.[6] Another example of these poor exchange equivalents is that a mule load of shallots, or two large sacks, was worth the value of only four litres of vegetable oil, or some US$4 in 1990.

It will come as no surprise, then, that intensive haggling over every item, bought or sold, characterizes the activity in this market-place. The disparity in power between visiting merchants and local peasants in dictating prices is especially expressed in certain characteristic behaviour. *Cholo* merchants from the larger cities noisily try to make fast deals with their indigenous counterparts, while the latter remain rather tongue-tied. For example, in the case of animal sales, farmers prefer to act more slowly, hoping that the price offered for their animal will go up, while the merchants instead insistently try to rush a deal and bully their customers by announcing their imminent departure.[7]

While the market is taking place, announcements are made through loud-speakers installed in the tower of the Mission church. The theft or loss of some item is announced in Quichua, Spanish and sometimes in a Zumbahuan mixture of both. The representatives of the parish town itself, called 'Junta' (largely composed of a 'white' leadership), may announce a parish-wide collective effort to clean up the market space the following week. A new social force also makes its presence known through the loudspeakers: the UNOCIZ. This is the Union of Peasant and Indigenous Organizations of Zumbahua, which has existed since 1988 and seeks to represent Zumbahuan peasants and communities to the outside world. Having arisen in resistance to the local church authorities and the Junta, UNOCIZ currently tries to expand its power base by acting as mediator between all incoming development institutions and the indigenous villages of Zumbahua. It also seeks to unify and strengthen the area's farmers as a united political force in order to formulate and more successfully demand state services for the parish.

By noon, when the first merchants start packing up their belongings and the numerous food stalls run out of their highly prized culinary delicatessen such as chicken soup, fried fish or potato tortillas, the market finally quietens down. The crowd slowly thins out and drunken men glower fiercely at bypassers or cry heartrendingly over some family misfortune.[8] By one o'clock the market activity is definitely over. Most people move off with loads of food or a tank of cooking gas tied to their shoulders. A few drunks remain behind, leaning on a house wall trying to recover their sobriety, watched over by young daughters or grand-daughters who wait patiently beside them. The whole market-place is covered with refuse and the strong smell of sugar-cane liquor permeates the air.

Ecology and economy

In geographic terms, the parish of Zumbahua consists of a broad, dry plain in the midst of a steep, rugged and eroding mountain terrain which reaches a height of 4500 metres in its southern part. The climate throughout the parish is cool to cold all year round; hail and frost are always a danger to agriculture. An ex-employee of the former hacienda of Zumbahua pin-pointed the climatic situation as follows: nature in Zumbahua behaves chaotically. The dry season usually begins in June and ends in September, offering deep blue, sunny skies but also clear frosty nights, storms and dusty air. The rainy season begins in October with hailstorms and heavy rainfall. Until May the sky is often cloudy, and if sunny days do occur they often precede night frosts. These frosts are especially feared by the farmers because they can be disastrous for their ripening crops.

Three life zones lie within the parish. The Ecuadorian ecologist Cañadas (1983), following Holdridge (1967), classified the first two which are the most extensive, as 'moist forest Montane' and 'wet forest Montane', respectively. Average annual temperature of both zones is between 6–12°C, while annual rainfall ranges between 500 to 1000 mm in the former and more than 1000 mm in the latter. A third zone is called 'wet forest Subalpine' characterized by an average annual temperature of only 3–6°C and 500 to 1000 mm yearly rainfall. These three zones represent more than 83 per cent of Ecuador's entire *paramo* area (calculation based on Cañadas 1983: 165–78).

Agricultural production systems roughly correspond to these three 'life zones'. The first and lowest in altitude (3500 m) produces principally barley, tubers, beans, and tiny plots of *quinoa*, *chochos* and peas. Garlic is the primary cash crop in this zone. This production mainly takes place in a dry plain at the centre of the parish where irrigation can be practised only in small pockets reserved for cash crops.

A second production system is found higher up on the steep slopes on the southern rim of the Zumbahuan central plain. Here the most important commercial crop is shallots with some garlic. Peasants also grow tubers and beans and a variety of livestock, – though pasture land is very limited. Irrigation channels leading water down to the plain criss-cross this area, but only some smaller fields are irrigated here, mostly those with cash crops planted on them.

The third and highest production zone starts at an altitude of approximately 3800 m. This zone is covered by natural grass and used extensively for animal husbandry. In terms of numbers and utility, the most important grazing animals are sheep, providing their owners with milk, wool, meat, dung and, of course, monetary income through sales. Additionally, llamas, pigs, cattle, donkeys, mules and horses also forage the grasslands.

Table 1: Average family income in Michacala, 1989

Productive sector	Annual Income (in US$)*	(in %)
Cropping	195	36
Animal	97	18
Wage labour	164	30
Trade	87	16
Total	543	100

Source 3
*US$1 = 576.7 sucres in 1989; see Banco Central del Ecuador 1989–90.

The poverty of the rural areas is pervasive throughout the parish of Zumbahua. Temporary migration for supplemental family income has therefore become increasingly common for most parish men since the dissolution of the hacienda system in 1964. In an economic evaluation of the income composition of Michacalan households, we found that approximately half of the average cash income per year stems from temporary employment and trade in both highland and coastal cities and only the remainder from agricultural sales (Table 1). The Michacalan data reflects, in our opinion, the situation of most other parish communities.

Our questionnaire revealed that in 1989, 81 per cent of all Michacalan families sent at least one man to earn cash as a day labourer on construction sites or as a porter in the markets, mainly in Ecuador's capital, Quito. Michacalan fathers spend an average of four to five months a year in Quito, Quevedo or La Maná. In that time they can generate more income for their families than by agricultural production in the village during the whole of the rest of the year. Still their total annual earnings amount to only US$540, which must cover the needs of five family members. This, then, corresponds to a per capita income of US$110, roughly one-ninth of the national average GNP per capita of US$1040 in Ecuador in 1987–9 (Europe World Year Book, 1992).

A typical migrant from Michacala will live for some weeks in rough wooden barracks right next to the construction site, or more usually, in the concrete basement of the site itself, surviving on a diet of bread and coca-cola, potatoes and bean soup. He will work 10 to 12 hours a day, five or six days a week, and will be paid the legal minimum wage of 45 000 sucres (US$78). He will receive no employment insurance or guarantee of any kind. At night he will tuck himself under his *poncho* and sleep on top of layers of cardboard and newspaper. But when he leaves the site on Sunday, most likely with a friend, he will face pleasures and dangers never experienced back home. Prostitutes will try to relieve him of his meagre earnings, cars will speed through the streets ignoring the pedestrians, thieves will attack people even in the middle of the crowded market-place. Ambulances – he may well wonder what sort of cars these are – will screech through the main streets. After several weeks he will pack his bags, collect his savings, buy some treats for his children and return home, only to find himself forced to leave again in search of work a few weeks or months later.

History of Zumbahua

In Zumbahua, farming takes place higher up than anywhere else in Ecuador (Gondard, 1986; Hess, 1990). Some areas are 3900 m above sea-level, yet expansion upwards has still not ended. In prehispanic times, however, all of what is now the parish of Zumbahua was well above the upper limit of agricultural production and covered in its entirety by the typical vegetation of the Andean *paramos*, namely bunch grasses and cushion plants. In the second half of the seventeenth century, these natural grass lands were sold by the Spanish Crown to the Augustinian Order and became a hacienda dedicated to sheep and wool production (Zúñiga, 1980: 189–90). A century later the hacienda of Zumbahua produced some 90 000 pounds of wool (Carrera, 1981: 115). This is an impressive quantity and makes a rough estimate of the sheep population possible as one good sheep shear might then have weighed some three to four pounds. This would mean a sheep population of between 20 000 and 30 000 – more sheep than are there today. This also means that the hacienda territory must have been pasture land with only small areas dedicated to crop production. The indigenous labour force performing herding tasks for the Augustinians was probably quite small. By the nineteenth century, the hacienda of Zumbahua had changed to a mixture of agriculture and animal husbandry producing barley, potatoes and beans in larger quantities, in addition to wool and cheese (Sources 1 and 5).

What seems to have occurred between the seventeenth and nineteenth centuries is that the Augustinians, following the general custom of hacienda owners in colonial and early republican times, secured a stable work-force for their hacienda not by paying wages, but by allocating a certain amount of land within the hacienda, called 'the entrance to the house' (Quichua: *huasipungo*). This land was used for subsistence agriculture by anybody willing to work for the hacienda.[9] With the passage of time and a growing number of labourers, an ever greater amount of the hacienda territory was transformed from natural grasslands into agricultural plots. The best land, that is, the most fertile and level land, was reserved for agricultural use by the hacienda itself, while lands farther away, on steep slopes or high on the mountain tops were assigned to the indigenous labour force.

In 1908, the hacienda of Zumbahua, as well as most other church land estates, were expropriated under the liberal government of Eloy Alfaro by way of the '*Ley de Beneficencia*'. The huge haciendas became state administered but were usually rented out to private entrepreneurs for several consecutive years. With the rents from the haciendas, the state financed social programmes in the cities, like medical services and orphanages. The agrarian reform of 1964 and the second reform of 1973 affected these state haciendas most and, to a lesser degree, also the privately owned haciendas. In the case of Zumbahua, the indigenous work-force had never been paid any salaries. They received their *huasipungos* and rations of agricultural produce as compensation for labour on the hacienda. Yet, it was possible for the indigenous workers to borrow money from the hacienda treasurer in the event of a religious celebration, a wedding or for emergency expenses.

Local lore has it that the land on which the community of Michacala sits today was lost to a private owner by the Augustinian monks through gambling many years ago. Whatever the truth is, since time immemorial until 1910, Michacala was indeed a private hacienda belonging to the family Estupiñan in Latacunga. This hacienda constituted a curious exception in a region where all other land was controlled by religious societies. The last owner, childless, old and perhaps impressed by the wave of hacienda expropriations that had occurred under the first liberal president, Eloy Alfaro, stipulated in his will that Michacala and two of his other haciendas be used to fund an asylum for the elderly poor in

Latacunga (Source 6). The foundation managing the asylum later sublet these haciendas and financed their social services with the rents they received until these properties were expropriated by the agrarian reform of 1964.

Although Michacala has been independent of the larger hacienda at Zumbahua, it has always been closely related to it. Unlike Zumbahua, the hacienda of Michacala was dedicated exclusively to cattle and sheep production. It was never an important hacienda in terms of the profit it brought to its owners; so unimportant was it that none of its temporary lessees or even any of its administrators ever actually bothered to live there. The only ones living within its territory were the indigenous work-force comprising a dozen or so *huasipungueros*, and *yanaperos*.[10] An overseer (Spanish: *mayordomo*) turned up once a week to assign the labour that had to be carried out by the indigenous people, now, in effect, serfs. These assignments included taking care of the animals, feeding salt, branding, castrating, curing sheep and cattle, collecting cows' milk and making cheese.

Even though sheep and cattle were the prime production choice of this hacienda, the indigenous labour force did, of course, work tiny plots assigned to them. Furthermore, most of the Michacalan *huasipungueros* entered into share-cropping relations with relatives on the neighbouring hacienda of Zumbahua in order to share the produce. All Michacaleños also had private flocks of sheep and llamas, and in fact, many Michacaleños insist that they were much larger then than they are today.

The agrarian reform in 1964 brought drastic changes to the way of life of Michacalan people. According to a report by a state official who visited the area in 1967 to prepare the legal transition of the hacienda to its indigenous work-force, Michacala had still a pastoral focus. He writes: 'The subsistence base is the breeding of wool animals, because the Indians live in grasslands that are not suited for any cultivation' (Source 4). To a certain extent, local people gained power over their lives, time and land. Additionally, they started to reorient their whole economy. They expanded their agricultural production, especially of the cash crop: shallots. The men, no longer bound to serve the hacienda for specified periods of time, soon began to migrate temporarily in search of additional income. Since then Michacala has rapidly developed into a community that is strongly integrated into the regional and national labour and food markets.

We were told by an ex-employee of the hacienda administration that the size of the *huasipungos* in Zumbahua as well as in Michacala ranged from one to 10 hectares.[11] Differences in size apparently depended on the amount of labour provided by the family to the hacienda; the more labour an indigenous family provided, the more land it received for its services, at least in theory. Of course only the hacienda decided to whom to accord land and which land to give. When the hacienda had finally disappeared after the agrarian reform in 1964, its ex-serfs' variously sized huasipungos became their private property while the hacienda's remaining grasslands became communal property. Thus the various hacienda settlements within the territory of the former hacienda, called in Spanish *sectores*, turned into *comunidades*, some only nominally and others legally, recognized by the Ministry of Agriculture.

Ever since, average family landholding within these communities was (and still is) shrinking, due to population growth and divisions within peasant families. A leader of Zumbahua's indigenous peasant organization (UNOCIZ) estimated that, in 1990, each family in the parish held roughly an average of 3.5 hectares of cultivable land. Nevertheless, the differences in landholding among peasant villages, as well as within specific villages, can be marked. For example, the fringe areas of the parish are less densely populated than the central part, and still retain considerable communal grassland. One must bear in mind, however, that due to the very high altitude, harsh climate and topography, agricultural productivity is far lower than in many other highland areas of Ecuador.

All the inhabitants of Zumbahua prefer mixed agro-pastoral production for the following reasons. The lower agricultural communities, lacking natural pasture, nevertheless have a high demand for animal dung, without which sustained agriculture, and potato production in particular is impossible.[12] The soil is generally low in phosphorus and nitrogen, micro-elements indispensable for plant growth and production. In turn, chemical fertilizer is too expensive to be a real alternative to animal dung. We once calculated that the amount of fertilizer necessary for one hectare field of potato would cost US$225, or more than 40 per cent of the entire average family income per year in Michacala in 1989 (Hess, 1992: 136). For the members of pastoral communities owning vast amounts of natural grassland, on the other hand, a mixed agricultural strategy is also indispensable because of the surprisingly low productivity and profitability of their livestock economy, as we will show later in the case study of Michacala.

Yamamoto (1985) has correctly pointed out that crop and animal producing communities are often treated as independent entities, while in reality the interconnection between both production types may be not an option but a necessity, in order to attain self-sufficiency. To serve the needs of both kinds of communities, the Zumbahuan people have elaborated a regional system that allows pasture-poor peasants to keep their animals in communities with reserves of natural pasture during most of the year, retrieving them only for manuring their own fields. Host communities with extensive natural pasture, but fewer arable fields are given barley, potatoes and beans in return for looking after other people's animals. They are never given a share of animal offspring. Additionally, they may also acquire arable land through share-cropping (Spanish: *al partir*; Spanish/Quichua: *partincapac*) with kin and friends who live in crop-producing communities and who reward their herding activities.

The existence of similar exchange systems involving either products or natural resources has been reported over and over again for the Peruvian Andes (Brush, 1977; Custred, 1974; Tomoeda, 1985), while little has been done in this respect in the ethnographically less explored territory of Ecuador. The peculiarity here is that similar exchange systems which 'equalize resources' – to use Guillet's words – exist in such geographically small areas. This kind of control over complementary eco-zones so close to each other that they are within one day's travel was termed by the ethno-historian Udo Oberem (1978) 'microvertical' economy.[13] In the case of Zumbahua, people exchange access rights to agricultural land for access rights to pasture land. The exchange system is based on kinship and marriage ties and is expanded through the establishment of assumed kin relations between *compadres*.

The community of Michacala

In terms of area, Michacala is one of the largest of all Zumbahuan communities, occupying a total of 4800 hectares on the uppermost reaches of the Toachi River. It is the southernmost community of the parish and also one of its highest, ranging from 3700 to 4400 metres. In demographic terms, however, Michacala is one of the smaller villages. In 1990, it had only 656 inhabitants, members of 134 families.

Child mortality is extraordinarily high in Michacala. Since about 1950, every third or fourth child dies before reaching the age of one. The major causes of child death have been lung diseases, measles and whooping cough, and gastroenteric infections. Child mortality is a frequent cause of severe emotional stress in Michacalan families. A villager once explained that parents try to avoid getting emotionally involved with their new babies, especially during the first weeks. She told us that this was out of fear of being overwhelmed by grief if the child should die.

In Michacala, child mortality during the first year of life is four times higher than the national average.[14] This extremely high rate may explain a low yearly population increase of 1.3 per cent in the village for the period between 1965 and 1990, while the national average was as high as 2.9 to 3.1 per cent (CONADE 1987: 17). Michacala's comparatively low growth rate does not result from steady emigration. In fact, only four families have left Michacala during the last two decades – to live in Quito most of the year. But even they have retained their status as villagers and usually leave their land and animals in the care of relatives.

Michacala is some seven kilometres from the parish town of Zumbahua. It is accessible only by an unpaved road diverging from the main road about a mile before Zumbahua proper, which is always in dreadful condition. After passing through the community of Huantopolo, the road narrows into a path that soon enters a steep gorge cut into a rocky ridge some 100 metres high. This ridge seals off the upper valley of the Zumbahua River from its lower part, which slopes down to the Zumbahuan plain. In the lower section of the gorge, alongside a noisy yellow-reddish creek, grow patches of low silver-leafed *quishuar* trees and reed-like grasses. The gorge, known by the name Huayama (swallow bird), is a wind channel and those who walk along it have to fight their way up the trail. The path winds up the northern wall of the gorge. Climbing slippery steps, one has to carefully avoid its sharp edge, which falls abruptly away some 30 metres at its highest point. From the bottom of the gorge one still faces an arduous 40-minute climb up to the centre of Michacala village.

Leaving the gorge behind, one is suddenly faced with the narrow entrances of two valleys, one to the east and the other to the south, separated by the steep flanks of Sunirumi, one of the highest peaks within Michacalan territory. At the upper edge of a plain stretching out at the foot of this mountain is a small cluster of buildings. This is Michacala's civic centre. In the foreground are shallot gardens surrounded by thick and high earthen walls, called *zanjas*. Other fields, planted with tubers and beans, cling to the mountainsides all around. But in general *paramo* vegetation prevails, that is, ground-level herbage and bunch grasses.

The centre of Michacala has only a concrete Catholic chapel with a tiny unpaved plaza in front, three communal buildings and two small shops. Basic foodstuffs are sold: noodles, rice, salt, sweets, some generic medicines, matches, soft drinks and, most important for social get-togethers, liquor. The village centre is clearly dominated by two, quite recently built but already dilapidated, school buildings.

Michacala got its first primary school in the 1970s, but formal education – especially for girls – still remains a low priority for most parents. Adult men often told us that they were illiterate because their parents did not like to send them to school when they were young. Others had dropped out early of their own accord because in those times they still 'could not think correctly' (Quichua:

mana alli yuyashcami). Even today, many villagers think that school education is for rich and lazy white children but not for their own offspring. None the less, attendance at primary school has markedly increased, even though the dropout rate is still very high. The schoolteachers reported that the majority of pupils stay for three years, or 'until they can sign their names'.

The village centre is lively only when school is on, on Mondays when the communal work parties meet, or when some migrant returning from the city stops by with friends for several shots of *tragu* (liquor). One Sunday each month a Catholic priest arrives to baptize children and marry couples in the chapel.

Three broad, flat valleys open up very near the village centre. Their bottoms are covered with cushion plants, while on the sides grow yellow bunch grasses (Quichua: *mama ucsha*). These three valleys taken together constitute the central feature of Michacalan geography.

In looking out over these valleys, one can see numerous green shallot gardens surrounded by *zanjas*. Close to them, clinging to the side slopes of the valley, are clusters of small houses. These are residential compounds containing several houses each, generally built in a variety of construction styles.

The most common is the *chaqui huasi* (foot house), made entirely of local materials. It is basically a straw hut whose floor has been dug half a metre below the ground. The structure itself is made of thick, bowed trunks of *quishuar* trees and a grid of thin branches, thatched with *paramo* grasses. The second most common style is the *adobe huasi*, which is made of earthen bricks locally mixed with loamy earth, short-cut grasses and water that have been moulded and dried for a week in the sun. A third house type has massive thick mud walls (Spanish: *tapiales*), and is the most durable kind of house structure. A moist mud mixture is poured into a wooden mould and dried for several weeks before the next patch of wall is moulded. The whole is roofed with a grass thatch or with zinc. There are even a few 'city style' houses in Michacala, made of concrete blocks and cement plaster and topped with zinc roofs. These proclaim the affluence of their owners. Despite a growing interest in building at least one modern home, most Michacalan families use them only for storage, while the traditional houses are the ones the families actually live in.

All houses are fairly small (some two by two and a half metres) and usually windowless. A majority of Michacalan families own at least two of them, a cooking hut where most family members will also sleep at night, and a second for storage. The cooking hut is the centre of family life. It is covered entirely with a thick layer of grasses and is therefore very dark inside, and made even darker by soot from the open cooking fire. The fireplace can be found in one of the corners. It is composed of two stones holding three iron bars. Several blackened pots stand close by.

There is little furniture to be found in these houses: perhaps a few tiny wooden benches and a wooden bed frame. The whole family's clothing may lie on the bed, rags, and belts, left there during the rush of early morning dressing. Some huge wooden spoons and long leather ropes usually hang along the wall. On a wooden shelf near the fireplace are cups, plates, a bottle with cooking oil, a handful of shallots, a kerosene candle, an old knife which is used for peeling potatoes, and perhaps a bag of salt. On the floor close to the shelf is a large grinding stone for barley and some corn varieties imported from lower areas that are the basis of every meal.

From one of the roof poles may hang a string of 10 egg shells already blackened from the fire. They remain there from the last time the female owner of the cooking hut gave birth, when raw eggs were mixed in a barley drink for her to 'cool down' her body temperature. A spindle attached to a ball of wool is stuck in the lower part of the grass roof. The entrance door, which is actually more of a barrier to keep animals and thieves out, does not prevent the icy wind from entering.

We learned that nearly half the village families own from three to five houses, most of which are used to store all sorts of tools, seeds and blankets, sheep shears, ropes, sacks, saddles and dancing costumes for festivals. Large wooden boxes normally contain the most valuable and perishable things a family owns, such as pictures, IDs, birth certificates and certain festive clothes. On a wall may hang an old rifle, some fox tails and a picture of a saint or the Virgin Mary.

Labour organization

Nuclear families are the primary units of consumption in Michacala. A nuclear family is a married couple living with children. Extended families are nuclear ones as defined above plus one or more adopted children (Quichua: *huiña-chishca*), unmarried siblings, a widowed parent of one of the spouses, or other relatives living with the family on a permanent basis and sharing all meals. Besides being a consumption unit, nuclear and extended families are the primary political units within the communal organization. Each unit has equal rights and obligations towards the village and each has only one vote in the communal assembly, no matter the number of its adult members.

While nuclear and extended families are consumption and political units, the productive units are composed of at least two to five nuclear families that together make up a compound. Compounds are both physical and social entities in Michacala.

The physical structure of a compound is a cluster of huts built close to each other, plus at least two animal corrals (Quichua: *quincha*), one for sheep and goats and the other for llamas. Behind most clusters one can find several tiny caves dug into the ground, called pig's nests (Quichua: *cuchi quisha*), whose bottom is bedded with *paramo* grass. Here, one or two pigs sleep at night. Next to the corrals there are always several dung heaps (Quichua: *huanu tanta-chishca*), often covered with plastic sheets to protect them from being washed away by heavy rain.

As a social unit, the compound nearly always centres around a parent couple who arrange the daily chores with at least one of their married children or a married sibling of one of the spouses. Ideally, the structuring principle underlying compound composition is patrilocality after a short period (perhaps a few years) of matrilocality immediately after the marriage. Nowadays, post-marital residence seems to depend much more on the relative size of the agricultural plots owned by the parents of the groom compared to those owned by the parents of the bride than on any fixed rule of patrilocality. A recently married couple is most likely to build their own cooking hut within the compound of whichever set of parents can – or will – offer them the biggest share of land to start their own subsistence production. It is often only the youngest child of a couple, regardless of sex, that continues to live with the parents until old age; all other children aim to form compounds of their own within several years of getting married.

Complex inter-family labour organization has always been considered a particular characteristic of Andean societies (Golte, 1980; Mayer and Bolton, 1980).

Many observers have argued that the tight limits of production imposed by nature in terms of ecology and agricultural productivity, could only be offset in the Andes by developing an extensive and reliable organization of inter-family labour loans. Most mutual help in Michacala involves families of the same compound, and this is the reason for considering compounds and not families as the prime units of production, even though all means of production (tools, animals, plots) are the private property of the nuclear or extended family and do not belong to the whole compound.

Women cook, take care of the children and wash their family clothes in the icy river, but their contribution is not restricted to domestic duties. In the Andes women are in charge of all small livestock production. This fact is often ignored by development projects which mainly target the male population (Fernandéz, 1992). Women substitute for men in almost every male task, as the men are absent from the village for an average of four to five months per year. In this case they hoe, participate in communal work groups, load pack animals, or dig up shallots. Only a few tasks remain exclusively in the male domain, such as carrying harvests home from the fields or rounding up wild cattle in the high *paramo*. Also, only men castrate animals like steer or horses or free-range pigs. This is because male strength is considered indispensable for these tasks, which require not only physical strength but also courage (Spanish: *coraje*). Females are considered to have less of these qualities. Men's primary task nowadays is unquestionably that of finding additional income for their family through temporary work stays in distant cities or trade. The men's frequent absence from their homes has added considerably to the work-load of women who remain in the village and provide for the family alone.

Men, on the other hand, have experienced a recent increase in their power within the marital relationship because of their cash. Moreover, migration has forced them to know more about the outside world and to speak Spanish, thus reinforcing their traditional position of principal mediators between the community and the outside world. These trends are further accentuated by the activities and attitudes of both national and international development agencies, which normally address only men as the decision-makers. All this has negatively affected women's participation, their structural position in the village context, and the cultural value placed on their contributions all over the Andes (Bourque and Warren, 1981).

The growing imbalance in the work-load between the sexes in Michacala is also reflected in the fact that young girls have had to contribute significantly more to the family economy than their brothers and much earlier on in their lives. In general, young girls watch over toddlers when their mothers have to be out. They also tend the family flocks much more often than their brothers. They are generally a great help to their mothers, which is why Michacalan women wish for girls as their first child. Girls, unlike boys, either do not attend primary school at all or else attend school for fewer years than their brothers because they are needed for household duties and to tend animals. On average, male students drop out of school at age 12 or 13 when they begin to accompany their fathers to work in the cities. The little money that they earn, they can spend on a new pair of trousers, shoes or even a watch, while their sisters will never have any money of their own until they are married and can sell their own products.

Villagers preferably ask close family members for *prestamano* (Quichua: *maquita mañana*), and assumed kin such as *compadres* who happen to live nearby.[15] Those who give a hand are fed by the family they work with during the work day. During harvest, they may also receive a share of the produce as a compensation for their labour. The amount of what they receive depends on the overall volume of the harvest. That is, if a harvest is slim, helpers receive nothing at all, while after a good harvest, their shares are generous.[16]

The interdependence of families and compounds in Michacala does not end with demands on labour. Kin also constitute consumption and exchange networks. Baskets of potatoes, portions of butchered animals, sweets, fruits, money and information as well as hungry stomachs move incessantly back and forth from the fireplaces between residential units. Therefore, a poor family is – as in most Andean communities – not just a family lacking property but a family with few relatives. By saying '*ñuca huacchallami causani*' or 'I live poorly', villagers indicate that they have no or few children and relatives. Such a concept of poverty clashes head on with the one that informs most development questionnaires or surveys.

Kin

Given the practical and social importance of kin, it is no wonder that the more kin a person has, the more they will be respected by the other villagers. This rule of thumb applies to real as well as assumed kin. Villagers without a large family feel prone to attacks by other villagers as they have nobody to defend them against criticism or injury. Real and assumed kinship are the basis for defence and protection whether an accused is at fault or not. This is the reason why it is so common to hear individuals who have married into Michacala from other localities complaining that their co-villagers do not respect them; a state of affairs they consistently blame on the fact that their relatives live too far away to defend them. As one embittered villager once said to us, 'If my brothers lived here, Michacaleños would not dare to talk to me like that!'

Personal well-being and a villager's sense of security, then, depend strongly on the proximity and overall number of kin. The importance of this pre-condition for an individual's physical, emotional and social well-being is expressed in a constant striving by all Michacaleños to expand their kin system beyond its blood basis, as well as beyond pure economic necessity, by selecting multiple types of godparents for their children.

In fact, each child in Michacala has not just one set of godparents but as many as three. The first godfather or godmother of a child, called *sarun taita* (ancestor), or *sarun mama* (ancestress) in Quichua, is chosen by the parents shortly after birth, generally from among the people who come to visit the new-born and mother. During a brief ceremony, the godparent gives the baby a name, prays for him and symbolically baptizes him. It is considered a special honour to be asked to become *sarun taita* or *sarun mama*, as villagers believe that the child will acquire the personality traits of this type of godparent. To be asked to be a *sarun taita* or *mama* means that the parents of the new-born consider you a highly worthy person whose character and disposition they want passed on to their child.[17]

The second pair of godparents is chosen roughly a year later. They are asked to take the child to the church, where it will be baptized. These godparents are called *llucshi mama* and *llucshi taita*, meaning 'the mother and father who are taking [the child] away'. A third and most important type of godparents are, finally, those who actually hold the child in church, during its baptism. They will pay for the baptismal clothes, and after the celebration will invite the child's family to their home for a feast. They also often pay for a band to entertain their guests for two or three days in a row.

The third and most important pair of godparents is called *achi mama* and *achi taita*. We attempted to find a translation for *achi*, but the villagers had no explanation other than 'that is just how it is called'. Dictionaries helped to clarify the meaning of '*achik*', or '*achic*', meaning 'enchanted with' or 'illuminated' (Torres, 1982; Cordero, 1989. The first meaning would imply the spiritual relationship between godparents and child, in the same sense we mentioned for the *sarun taita* or *mama*, namely that personal qualities are passed on to the child. The second meaning reminds us of the customary procedure, during Catholic baptisms, of lighting and holding a candle while calling for the enlightenment of the child and his or her godparents.

All three types of godparents are expected to give small gifts of food to their godchild from time to time. Moreover, they are obliged to help their godchild's natural parents whenever asked. Godparents are also expected to side with their godchild's family in any conflict, and never to offend or insult them. These moral expectations are clearly expressed in a local usage that is often made during emotional declarations when *compadres* say with gratitude to each other: 'We are like one hand, one mind, one heart'. In Quichua this is: '*nucanchiclla shuc maqui, shuc yuyai, shuc shuncu canchic*'.[18] This symbolic relationship of brother- and sisterhood is also expressed in the taboo on marriage between widowed *compadres*.[19] It mirrors the taboo that a man shall not marry the widow of his brother.

Through *compadrazgo*, the total of family relations of any member of the indigenous community ranges far beyond those kin living within one's own and neighbouring compounds. Gudeman (1971) distinguishes between horizontal and vertical ways of extending one's kin relations through *compadrazgo*. By horizontal extensions he means godparent relationships as established between social equals. By vertical extension, he refers to family relations established across social-class levels. Michacaleños seek to establish both types of relationships in a complementary fashion. To have at least some distant, higher ranking *compadres* is considered advantageous because they may be in a position to offer food, gifts and services that a local *compadre* cannot. But there are also disadvantages: distant *compadres* cannot lend a hand in daily chores, lend a draught animal or help bury a relative the way local ones can. Moreover, a far-away *compadre* cannot defend a person against verbal criticisms or in fist fights with other villagers.

Agrarian structure

At present there are three kinds of access rights to land in Michacala. There is privately owned land (totalling 140 hectares), group land (totalling 20 hectares) and communal pasture land (some 4600 hectares). Communal pasture and private holdings are the result of the agrarian reform of 1964. Since then the private plots have been inherited and partitioned by the children of the former serfs. Additionally, any family formed after the expropriation of the hacienda could and still may apply to the communal council for a plot of land of their own. These plots are carved out of the communally held pasture area, allowing their owners to start agricultural production, especially the production of shallots. Thus, small chunks of communal pasture, mostly located in the humid pampas, have continuously been assigned to individual families which treat them as their private property.

All privately owned land in Michacala itself is dedicated to shallot production (roughly 50 hectares), to tubers[20], beans and a little barley. Michacaleños own an

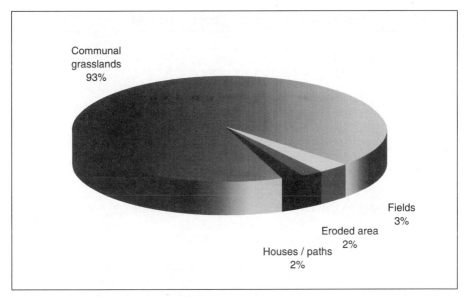

Figure 1   *Land use in Michacala, 1990, in percentages*

additional 80 hectares of land in various neighbouring villages. These land-holdings are the result of inheritance and marriage by Michacaleños to partners from other villages. As these fields are generally located at much lower eleva-tions, they are eagerly sought after by the villagers for the production of a highly desired and scarce crop in the community: barley. All privately owned landhold-ings amount to an average of only 1.7 hectares per family, of which some 25 per cent are allowed to lie fallow every year.

The average of 1.7 hectare of farm land per family is indicative of the Michacalan situation, but is grossly insufficient in a *paramo* environment to support any family by agriculture alone. To illustrate this point, let us suppose that the average harvest on this land per family and per year is 14 *quintales* of tubers, three *quintales* of barley and two *quintales* of dried beans. These quan-tities are enough for a family of five for a maximum of just four months, meaning that two-thirds of all food consumed in the village every year must be purchased in the market-place (Hess, 1992: 123).

Still, despite the importance of crops in Michacala, at present, some 93 per cent of the village territory is natural pasture land and communally owned. The proportional relationship between privately cultivated fields and communal grassland is illustrated in Figure 1 above.

Livestock economy

Michacaleños tend 10 different animal species on their vast communal grass-lands. Nearly every Michacalan family possesses guinea-pigs and sheep. An overwhelming majority own llamas. Fewer Michacalan families own pigs (68 per cent of all households) and chickens (52 per cent). Finally, only a minority of the villagers own horses, mules, donkeys (28 per cent of households), 'wild' cattle[21] (21 per cent) or goats (13 per cent).

As shown in Table 2, Michacalan sheep owners are not a homogeneous group in terms of their animals. For example, while very few families have no sheep at

Table 2:   Average animal holding per household, 1989

Species	Ø Numbers/ family	SD*	Subtotal, in numbers
Sheep	17	16.3	2262
Guinea-pigs	15	9.3	1950
Llamas	5	6.0	663
Pigs	2	2.8	234
Chickens	1	2.2	182
Horses, donkeys	1	1.1	117
Cattle	1	1.8	91

Source 3
*SD = Standard deviation; subtotals do not include boarded animals. McCorkle (1983) uses the term 'boarded' for animals taken care of by those not their owners.

all, one family owns 80 head. And while some families own no llamas, the largest private herd contained 38. Regarding guinea-pigs, there are inter-familial differences of up to 50, and in pigs up to 20 animals. Finally, only a minority of families own cattle, but those who do may possess up to 10 head. Generally, young families have far fewer animals of any species than the older residents. Moreover, income from labour migration allows men, and not women, to acquire their preferred animal species, such as a horse or cattle. Women, when buying an animal, would prefer a sheep, llama, donkey or pig. Thus, wage labour income has initiated a 'male' tendency to less use-related animal husbandry. To own horses and cattle is very much a 'macho' status symbol.

All animals are private property. A Michacalan herd, then, is composed of animals belonging to all members of a household. Some of those animals are considered the property of particular individuals who have the right to sell their animals whenever they wish; other animals are considered property of the entire family unit. Individually owned sheep, pigs and fowl can be used as emergency cash in case of sudden necessities. All horses and cattle are the private property of the male family heads.

Animal gifts to young children are considered a way of stimulating their interest in sheep raising. Thus the youngsters learn how to take care of and be responsible for animals. This is important for later when they are adults with their own animals. But it is also important because these children tend the family herd every day. Having their own animals in the herd is supposed to make them look after the herd better.

According to local standards, a family with more than 50 sheep and 30 llamas is considered well off. Only five out of 134 families in the village meet this local criterion of affluence.

But not only Michacalan animals graze on the communal pasture lands of this village. Nearly half of all families take care of at least some animals owned by members of other communities in the Zumbahua parish.[22] These animals spend several months or even the whole year in Michacala territory. They are called in Quichua '*huihua mincana*', that is, boarded animals. One-third of Michacalan families, for example, regularly care for sheep belonging to others. A slightly smaller number (28 per cent) take care of 'foreign' llamas. Boarded pigs and cattle are cared for by 13 per cent and 11 per cent, respectively, of village

Table 3: Private and boarded animals in Michacala, 1989

Species	Ø Numbers/family	Total, in numbers
Sheep	25	3224
Llamas	7	845
Pigs	2	260
Chickens	1	182
Horses, donkeys	1	169
Cattle	1	130
Goats	1	78

Source 3

households. Lastly, some Michacalan families care for entrusted horses and donkeys (9 per cent) or goats (7 per cent).

Boarding animals refers to the actions of people from outside Michacala, who are adding some animals to the herd of a relative who lives in the community of Michacala. The Michacalan family that agrees to take care of somebody else's animals must be periodically compensated by giving them small amounts of sweets, bread or staples for this effort. Family members may also be given the privilege of share-cropping land in the village of the animals' owners. Those caring for other people's sheep enjoy the right to use the milk of all ewes cared for. Furthermore, they will collect their charges' dung and also use boarded llamas and donkeys as beasts of burden if there is a need.

Sheep are most frequently boarded in Michacala. According to our questionnaire, 'foreign' sheep taken care of in the community totalled an impressive 962 head out of 3224 pastured in Michacala during 1990. By comparison, during the same period only 182 llamas were entrusted to Michacaleños, an average of slightly more than one per family. Finally, only 52 horses, donkeys and mules, 39 cattle, 39 goats and 26 pigs in Michacala were not owned by the villagers themselves.

In sum then, an impressive number of sheep, llamas and pigs populate the pastures of Michacala. Soon after dawn, dozens of llama herds are driven up to the high mountains where they will pass the day without supervision. In the afternoon, they will be brought down to lower places to spend the night in the corral, above all to avoid theft. After breakfast, those tending sheep, goats and other animals, mostly children or elderly women, go off to spend the day in the grasslands. In the higher areas of the village, free-ranging llamas, wild cattle and horses can be found spread over the landscape while pigs forage the humid valley plains and leave the swamp area uprooted. Still, the average herd size per family remains surprisingly low, even when boarded animals are included, as Table 3 illustrates.

Conclusion

The ubiquitousness of rural poverty should not let us forget that it condemns those who suffer it to a very stressful life and to a strong desire to improve their condition. In our view, this desire for substantial change has been too often played down in anthropological writings about the poor in the Andes. Many social scientists picture them as experienced farmers in possession of some highly adaptive methods of producing crops in a very harsh environment.[23] The hardship of their lives is said to turn them into conservatives who wish to avoid risk and preserve the status quo, as meagre as that may be. What is overlooked is that this status quo is characterized by poor health, poor nutrition, constant overwork and a lack of capital. Under such circumstances, risk avoidance is indeed a short-range strategy to be expected. But, it is one that only detracts from its practitioners' long-range aspiration of achieving substantial change for the better.

Starn (1991) has criticized the tendency among students of Andean societies to underestimate the degree of economic dissatisfaction felt by the people they study. Referring specifically to the Department of Ayacucho in Peru, he has argued that the rise of the Shining Path movement in the 1980s was possible only on the basis of the widespread support given to it by a rural population frustrated by poverty.[24] Starn asks why it is that this discontent has not found cogent expression in otherwise well-researched and culturally sensitive ethnographies about the area, written before the 1980s. His explanation is that recent anthropological studies of indigenous peoples in the Peruvian central and southern highlands have generally concentrated either on the unusual degree of adaptation of the Andean people to their harsh mountain environment, or else on the symbolic structures that mediate this adaptation.

Without wishing to deny the intrinsic value of much research concerning the inner logic and ecological functioning of Andean production systems,[25] we none the less maintain that all of our admiration for systems of 'vertical control of multiple eco-zones', 'reciprocity' and complicated 'exchange networks' has made us blind to the fact that the complexity and sophistication of the 'Andean rationality' delivers only the most precarious existence to its practitioners.

Recent events outside Peru testify to the amount of dissatisfaction most Andean farmers feel about their lives. In June 1990, 10 000 indigenous people of Ecuador paralysed the entire nation's transport system for five consecutive days, producing one of those historical moments James Scott (1990) described as breaching the boundary between 'hidden' and 'public' transcripts. Although this protest, organized by indigenous people across Ecuador and CONAIE,[26] had even been announced in the most prominent newspapers, its size took the nation completely by surprise. Frank (1991) explained that the shock felt by most urban Ecuadorians at the indigenous ability to stage such a massive protest successfully, ultimately derived from a hegemonic image of the indigenous farmers as being intrinsically passive, conservative and emotionally attached to a life-style of stubborn resistance to modernity.[27] This image made it virtually inconceivable to most people that those Indians were able to carry out a nationwide protest. When that protest did occur, most non-indigenous Ecuadorians felt not only surprise, but their very picture of indigenous personality was suddenly called into question. Many tried to remain faithful to their original cast of mind by blaming the event on non-indigenous communist agitators – against all evidence (Frank, 1991). Frank's thesis (1992a, 1992b) allows us to identify the tendency of many post-1960s anthropological studies, to misrepresent the indigenous peasantry of the Andes as culturally conservative and passive, as just another expression of a far more generalized misconception of indigenous people's attributes. Such ethnic misconception is often politically grounded as it allows ethnic differences to be turned into tools for social and economic discrimination. Maybury-Lewis (1988) remarks: 'If we reexamine the role of ethnicity, particularly in Third World countries, we discover that allegations of ethnic divisiveness, backwardness, or separatism are often used by governments as cloaks for exploitation, authoritarianism, and hegemonic privilege' (p. 379).

Dissatisfaction with a life lived in poverty is not just our interpretation of the Zumbahuan condition. We wish to report one peculiarly Zumbahuan rebellious reaction against their painfully limited existence. Throughout the year, one can find sharp, bent nails scattered on the main road between Latacunga and Zumbahua. These nails are intended to puncture the tyres of cars coming up from the tropical coast and heading towards the Inter-Andean valley by way of the *paramos*. The punctured tyres are a nuisance to the drivers, especially when night falls and the *paramo* turns pitch black, freezing and foggy. Indigenous people enjoy these moments of empowerment as they watch unseen, the anxious car owners – symbolizing to them the rich – who otherwise would drive quickly through the area without stopping.

The principal question for Zumbahuan people then is: How can life be changed for the better? In this context, political parties, the Church and non-governmental organizations attempt to give them more options, mainly by helping to improve infrastructure and agricultural production. Much infrastructure, however, remains badly maintained and most of the technical suggestions to improve crop production are ignored by locals. Why does this happen; how and in which sense do development institutions fail?

We suggest that many projects fail because they largely ignore the communicative and cultural dimensions of their work. In our view, most developers seem to limit Andean culture to strange beliefs and customs as revealed, for example, during rituals or religious festivities. But, as long as they deal with mundane activities such as cropping, herding, fishing or the marketing of products, most seem to be convinced that they have reached a sufficiently down-to-earth level of pragmatic activity to be able to ignore the influence of culture altogether and to communicate as one agricultural professional to another. The view that mundane activities are culturally less endowed is not specific to developers, as even some anthropologists have the tendency to divide human life into sacred and profane spheres (for example, Durkheim) and prefer to concentrate on 'the sacred' as the real cultural one. Undeniably, the most applauded ethnographies are done on subjects such as headhunting (Rosaldo, 1980) or cock-fights (Geertz, 1973), and definitely not on agriculture.

4 Views on the environment

IN CHAPTERS 4 AND 5 we will present scientific and indigenous analyses of the conditions regarding cropping and sheep breeding in the *paramo* community of Michacala. The scientific study we are going to describe is the result of 30 months of interdisciplinary, quantitative research. It epitomizes very much the approach of our project, PROFOGAN. The indigenous appraisal aims to represent the local perspective on the agricultural production system, which we have produced from extensive qualitative research. The forthcoming ethnographic chapters document two distinct knowledge systems, which inform both culturally endowed analyses.

Our project research on the agro-pastoral economy in Michacala defined the basic limits to crop production as being primordially physical and biological ones, such as geography, climate and soil fertility. Social parameters such as labour and marketing arrangements were also considered important for determining productivity and profitability. This focus on physical and quantifiable aspects of the cropping system was logically the result of a culturally specific perspective derived from university-based agricultural sciences. Agronomic sciences define for development professionals how an agricultural system is constituted, and how it can be managed and improved: physical features of an agrosystem play a prominent role in that thought system.

Indigenous peasants, of course, also systematize their knowledge about agriculture. They too judge their cropping system through the particular lenses of an integrated set of ideas created by the social group in which they are born and educated. An indigenous knowledge system defines – as agroscience does for the developers – what kind of nature they are dealing with, which conditions limit a harvest, and how these interact. Both developers and farmers always have an idea as to what might solve the most immediate limits to agricultural production. Not surprisingly, then, we found that Michacalan people considered geographical, climatic and soil features to evaluate the situation of cropping, but these features alone do not deliver the ultimate explanation for a lean harvest. Additionally, indigenous peasants consider the influence of God, religious and supranatural forces to explain agricultural hazards or particularly abundant harvests.

If these interpretive differences as to how the agricultural process functions are noticed at all, developers immediately feel obliged to evaluate the local ideas they have stumbled upon, not on the basis of the local knowledge system they belong to, but on the basis of their own educational system. The result is often that local ideas fail the rationality test of experts. Chambers remarked that such a negative assessment is a rather generic phenomenon in development:

> From rich-country professionals and urban-based professionals in third world countries right down to the lowliest extension workers it is a common assumption that the modern scientific knowledge of the centre is sophisticated, advanced and valid and, conversely, that whatever rural people may know will be unsystematic, imprecise, superficial and often plain wrong. Development then entails disseminating this modern, scientific and sophisticated knowledge to inform and uplift the rural masses. Knowledge flows in one direction only – downward – from those who are strong, educated and enlightened, towards those who are weak, ignorant and in darkness.

(1983: 76)

This attitude has also often led to a serious undervaluation of local knowledge as technically less sophisticated. Since the late 1970s, IKS researchers have refuted such negative assessments' empirical data. Here, we will not even attempt to judge whether local or outsiders' knowledge is more correct in empirical terms. First, we do not have the technical know-how for such a final judgement. Second, and more importantly, we try to avoid defining experts' and farmers' knowledge as being either true or false, empirical or imaginative, as this would cut off the possibility for bridging the cognitive gap between their respective knowledge systems.

In other words, a formal university-based analysis of agricultural production must appear to indigenous peasants to be an incomplete analysis ignoring decisive religious and supernatural features. Moreover, as indigenous people cannot but evaluate the suggestions of developers, except on the basis of their own knowledge system, it is simply not reasonable to expect them to act on advice that is derived from a world view that rests on scientific parameters alone, leaving out an array of additional criteria that are part and parcel of their own theory and practice. This chapter will document the intricacies of scientific and indigenous appraisals concerning cropping and sheep husbandry.

A scientific view of nature

According to a scientific understanding of environmental conditions as they relate to agricultural production, an analysis must necessarily centre on geographical location, climate, altitude, topography and soil composition. These represent the most important conditions for crop production in any rural setting. Each of these parameters needs to be examined.

Climate and altitude

Temperature in Michacala is the result of the combination of altitude and the geographic position of the village in relation to the Equator. Since Michacala is located between 3700 and 4400 metres above sea-level and only 1.58° south of the Equator, a two-year reading of daily temperature revealed a monthly average of 7.7°C. with a variation of only two degrees (Figure 2).[1]

As far as agricultural productivity is concerned, the temperature regime in Michacala is clearly the most limiting factor of all when analysed from a scientific point of view. Low temperatures throughout the year and an irregular occurrence of night frosts slow down the growth rate and continuously threaten the survival of any cultivated crop throughout the production cycle. An average minimum daily temperature of 10°C is needed to guarantee normal plant growth and development in most species (personal communication, Cañadas). Average temperatures below this limit lead to serious delays in maturation, and may halt plant growth altogether.

In Michacala the mean temperature is only 7.7°C and agricultural productivity is understandably low in comparison with warmer areas of Ecuador. To determine maximum agricultural productivity per hectare, we gathered information from all Michacalan families. In the case of potatoes, the maximum harvest was said to be 6 tons/ha, which is two-thirds of the estimated average at the provincial level (MAG, 1989). Other tubers like *melloco*, *oca* and *mashua* were said to produce a maximum of 5.1 tons/ha and beans (in dried condition) 0.7 tons/ha. These optimal results for Michacalan conditions turn out to be only mediocre when compared to the average production of the same crops at the level of Cotopaxi Province (MAG,

1989). Only barley production does not seem to be negatively affected by the harsh Michacalan climate, since with 1.9 ton/ha, its results compared well with those on the provincial level. Shallot production, finally, can even be considered excellent in this community, reaching up to 16 tons/ha.

Given that the mean monthly temperatures are cool but relatively stable throughout the year, another climatic feature crucial in determining vegetation growth in Michacala is rainfall. Of special importance in this respect is not just overall quantity per year but the pattern of its distribution throughout the year.

According to the Holdridge system of life zones (1967), we have already mentioned that most of the Michacalan ecology is classified as 'humid forest Montane', which is defined by the combination of an average annual temperature of 6 to 12°C and 500 to 1000 mm yearly rainfall.[3] Combining temperature and rainfall data allows for the elaboration of an ombrothermic diagram (Figure 2). This diagram illustrates with low peaks a dry season occurring between June and September during which drizzles are, however, frequent early in the morning.

Ecologically speaking, a month is dry when evapo-transpiration is higher than precipitation (Gaussen, cf. Cañadas, 1983: 17). This was the case in Michacala only in September 1990 (Figure 2). Fortunately, such drought threatens Michacalan farming and herding only briefly each year, which means that vegetative growth in the village is nearly continuous.

Strong, cold winds characterize the high mountain environment of Michacala throughout the year, but they typically turn into destructive windstorms during the dry season from June to September. As the topsoil in the village is very dry during this period, these storms carry off a lot of earth, especially from places without a dense plant cover such as fallow fields. Sometimes during these

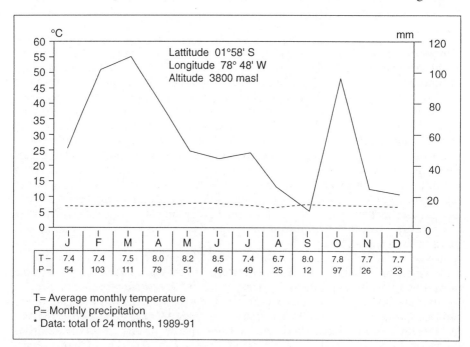

T= Average monthly temperature
P= Monthly precipitation
* Data: total of 24 months, 1989-91

Figure 2   *Ombrothermic Diagram of Michacala*
Source 9

months, the air becomes so filled with dust that breathing is difficult and the skin starts to burn under the needle-like impact of sand blowing on to the face.

Winds may also cause serious damage to crops, especially to those with elongated leaves like barley and shallots. Furthermore, strong winds may turn occasional burn-offs in the village's dry summer grasslands into uncontrollable blazes, leaving behind vast stretches of temporarily unusable pasture grounds which will subsequently be subject to increased erosion by more windstorms and after the dry period by heavy rainfalls.

Hail (Quichua: *runtu*) can fall any time of year in Michacala. Hailstorms are most frequent in October, during a time known as the *Condorazo de San Francisco*. This is the beginning of the rainy season, the time for planting, so that the frequent hail during this period does not seriously affect agricultural production. Hail may be highly damaging, however, when it occurs during the flowering time of the crops or when it hits mature crops with tall stalks, like barley and shallots, knocking them to the ground.

Finally, with average minimum nightly temperature as low as 2.2°C, frosts are another serious climatic risk to Michacalan crop production. Indeed, both indigenous farmers and agronomists consider frosts the most serious risk of all. Even though many scientific publications on *paramo* ecology (Parry, Knapp, Cañadas, 1987; Sarmiento, 1986; Cañadas, 1983) point out that northern Andean frosts occur most frequently during the arid season from June to September when clear skies prevail. They also occur during the rainy period. It is important to keep in mind that the humid season is the growing season of plants, meaning that frosts nearly always have devastating effects on the cultigens. It is true that with temperatures between 0 and –3°C, these frosts must be considered quite mild – especially when compared to those of the *altiplano* or *puna* areas of the southern Andes (Knapp, 1988: 184). Due to the much higher humidity of the air in the northern Andes, however, these mild frosts are sufficient to destroy entire leaf structures of cultivated plants.

By looking at the local climatic conditions alone, we conclude that the Michacalan territory is notably unsuited for crop production. And indeed, we encounter in Michacala the upper limit of any agriculture in Ecuador, namely up to 3900 m. The climatic odds seem to be such that significant improvement in crop production seems hardly viable and, ecologically, possibly detrimental. From an agro-technical perspective then, the Michacalan crop producers are hopelessly disadvantaged when compared to farmers in lower areas. They live on marginal territory and have to pay the relative costs of their location: highly risky and relatively low yielding.

Geography

After climate, agronomists note the terrain of Michacala as the second most important limiting factor for crop yields. The community can be characterized as overall vertical and steep. As already described, the village is made up of three valleys, divided by small but fast flowing creeks coloured yellow-reddish-brown due to the sediments of iron oxide and sulphur that are constantly being washed out of the mountains. These valleys are narrow at their openings but broaden into extended humid pampas (Quichua: *turu pampacuna*). Steep slopes enclose their semi-flat valley bottoms, densely covered with bunch grasses. Geology shows that these valleys were formed by glaciers which covered rock formations of volcanic and marine origin (Dirección General, 1978).

In the lower and warmer village sections, between 3700 and 3900 m, where production of tubers is risky but just possible, rocks and slopes of over 40 per cent incline predominate. Less steep areas here are used for shallot production. In the middle section of the valleys, on the other hand, at heights between 3800 and 3900 m, where the valley bottoms stretch out, high soil humidity prohibits agricultural use. Farming is therefore relegated to the slopes on both sides. But even though excessive humidity is not a problem on these slopes, their steep inclinations trigger severe erosion, when the natural grasscover has been tilled away or overgrazed. The serious consequences of wind and rain erosion are indeed already plain to see in numerous places.

In 1989, we estimated the area affected by severe erosion in Michacala to be over 200 hectares, most of it due to former agricultural activity, but some also due to overgrazing. Considering increasing demographic pressure and the relative decline of the value of local products versus purchased goods, it must be expected that the cultivated land dedicated to both cash crops and subsistence agriculture will expand further and accelerate erosion. Since 1987 villagers have made a collective effort to till stretches of virgin *paramo* land. Until now, these collective fields, covering in all some 20 hectares of steep mountain land, remain wholly unprotected against erosion.

The only seemingly anti-erosive measure taken by villagers has been the building of 3 m wall-ditches, called *zanjas*, which surround almost all shallot fields. Ecologists we have consulted say that they demonstrate excellent ecological expertise, reflecting the peasants' awareness of the dangers not only of wind and rain erosion, but also of the drainage problems of the humid pampas. The ecologists also believed that these walls were erected to prevent frost damage, as they influence the micro-climate on ground level positively.

For any agricultural professional, soil quality is a further determining factor for agricultural success in any environment. Therefore, the geological origin, soil consistency, water-retention capacities and acidity of Michacalan soils have been determined by the study of ecological maps and through consultation with a professional ecologist.

In general terms, most village soils are classified as black andean, franco-sandy to clay-rich, with an above-average capacity of water absorption which reaches up to 100 per cent in the flat areas. Two graduate students of agricultural sciences who worked with me during the first year of the investigation gathered five soil samples in different sites within Michacala to determine their chemical composition. The results show that the soils of Michacala contain sufficient amounts of organic matter but are slightly acidic (pH 5.6 to 6.2). Micro-elements are present in satisfying quantities, with the single exception of phosphorus. This specific micro-element is decisive, insofar as its absence is said to retard considerably plant growth.

Let us attempt a preliminary summary here. Advantages of the Michacalan ecology for crop and forage production are the quantity of rainfall and its quite regular distribution throughout the year. Yet the disadvantages are daunting: low overall temperature clearly restricts plant growth in cultivated as well as in natural vegetation species. Furthermore, climatic events like frosts, hail and storms threaten crop production frequently, rendering it highly risky even for root crops which are relatively well adapted to a cold climate.

As we have seen, soil quality is limited by the relative lack of phosphorus, slowing down overall productivity even more than the low temperatures. Maturation periods of tubers and beans are therefore explicably long in Michacala.

They need up to 11 months to be harvested. A shallot variety, called *cayambeña*, which is the fastest-growing crop species locally, still needs some seven months to mature before it can be harvested.

Furthermore, agricultural production on the steep slopes of Michacala must be considered ecologically ruinous to the village because it brings with it soil erosion. From an agronomic perspective, then, expanding agricultural production in a high-altitude economy like that of Michacala must include soil-protective measures and stop further sacrifice of the *paramo* grasslands for cultivation. Considering the ecological risks inherent to crop production without protection from erosion, we have suggested in a previous publication that development activities in *paramo* communities should focus on the improvement and promotion of animal husbandry (Hess, 1992: 149).

A Michacalan view of environmental forces

When Michacaleños look at their rugged mountain environment, they are aware of the same features as developers, but they interpret many of them differently. In what follows we try to give an introduction to how locals perceive their environment, and how it determines their daily lives and decisions. In the second part of the chapter, we take up the theme of agricultural productivity again and develop an indigenous theory of the causal link between agricultural yields and divine will.

Recently, Croll and Parkin have edited a book on the issue of indigenous people's relation to their environment, in which they remarked that: ' . . . the environment has often been isolated and observed by development specialists who bring their own distinctions, categorizations and knowledge to bear on it much as in another context the body has been subject to the clinical gaze' (1992: 28).

We have just presented an analysis of *paramo* environment based on such a clinical gaze. Making obvious that this specific gaze turns the Michacalan environment into a mechanical clockwork of features, events and properties basically unrelated to the human social sphere, even if knowledgeably malleable. The important feature here is that in a scientific interpretation there is no major causal moral relation between humans and their environment. Even though, according to a scientific understanding, certain human actions may be ecologically unwise and will backfire in the long run (for example, the ozone hole), such actions are considered at their worst imprudent but not morally reprehensible. It is only in a highly metaphorical sense that, in Western thought, certain ecological consequences triggered by human action can be identified as punishments. As we will show, however, in the Michacalan way of analysing their surroundings, such moral issues play a central role.

Michacaleños unquestionably love their mountainous homeland, despite all the hardship it forces on them. When asked about what is bad about living in other ecological zones of Ecuador they know, they admit that in lower-lying villages and especially in tropical areas, which they call 'wild land' (Quichua: *sacha allpa*), everything matures much faster and in larger quantities. Moreover, delicious fruits like bananas, oranges, cocoa and sugar-cane grow there, all of which are highly appreciated among Michacaleños because they are rare delicacies. However, most Michacaleños immediately add that living in these hot lands means suffering from heat and insects and falling sick easily.

In comparison, villagers appreciate the cool mountains that surround them, perceiving them to offer almost everything necessary for survival: crops, combustible materials with which to warm themselves and to cook, construction materials for shelter, and pasture for animals. So much do villagers respect their land that they often call it 'holy land' (Spanish: *Santa tierra*) or 'mother land' (Quichua: *mama allpa*). Even the natural pastures that surround them are some-times personalized and called 'mother grass' (Quichua: *mama ucsha*).

When further comparing their own village to other lower-lying villages, the Michacaleños never fail to point out that in Michacala there is still ample space. In other places, they insist, people have to live close to each other and they lack pasture for their animals. That is why people there so frequently fight over animals that trespass the boundaries of a neighbour's plot and damage crops. In densely settled villages, neighbours also take note of each other's activities, acquaintances and purchase of consumer goods. Therefore, people in such vil-lages are regarded as jealous, abusive and ready to quarrel with each other.

All this does not mean that Michacaleños regard the relationship with their mountain environment as completely free of tension. On the contrary, Michacaleños can point to a whole array of dangers prevalent within the village territory.

For example, we learned from a woman herding her family's animals that she has to watch over the animals carefully so as not to come into contact with 'rainbow water' (Quichua: *cuichi yacu*) or 'rainbow marshes' (Quichua: *cuichi turu pampa*). *Cuichi yacu* are water sources that shimmer in the sun in different colours, from the reddish-yellowish soils which abound in Michacala's humid valley bottoms. They are thought to have been touched by a rainbow, and turned thereby into an environmental feature highly dangerous to animals. Rainbows are, of course, a common occurrence in the *paramos* of Michacala, especially during the rainy season when drizzle often combines with sun beams. Animals, especially sheep, which drink the water touched by rainbows or graze where a rainbow has previously touched the ground may become sick and die (see also Chapter 5).

That Michacaleños experience their environment as a space that can threaten their lives or their animals is also documented by the taboo, which requires any woman who has recently given birth not to leave her hut for at least two weeks and often up to six weeks. This forces the husband to take over all female chores. His mother-in-law often helps out if she has time. Meanwhile, his wife rests on some layers of dry *paramo* grass, her head carefully wrapped in a warm shoulder cloth, and avoids any contact with the world outside her house.

Another expression of local knowledge about environmental dangers under-lay a question I was often asked by the villagers. Wasn't I afraid to walk through the entrance gorge of Michacala in Quichua called *Huayama?* At first I was very much puzzled about what danger they meant. Once or twice a year someone had a fatal accident in the gorge, slipping and falling, but usually these people were heavily intoxicated at the time. So what danger were people talking about? We will give the answer in a moment.

Still another example that illustrates the Michacaleños relationship with their environment is that they customarily carry a bottle of sugar-cane liquor along when they go to round up the semi-wild cattle, pigs and llamas grazing untended in more distant, higher *paramo* areas. We first thought that this was just to make a long and arduous walk up to the high mountain ridges more bearable. But far from it: the villagers' explanation for this habit is that a shot of cane liquor makes those who take it fearless and helps them to resist the wind and the mountain spirits.

According to the Michacaleños, the environment is alive with all sorts of dangers that emanate from different spiritual powers inhabiting, for example, certain (although not all) mountains, some (but not all) winds, and certain sites where paths, channels and rivers converge (Quichua: *tingu*). This sounds very similar to a report written by Crain (1991) on the folk cosmology of the northern Ecuadorian village in which she did her fieldwork:

> . . . many places that form part of the natural landscape are believed to be endowed with both positive and negative qualities. According to local belief, it is dangerous to walk or remain for an extended period of time near certain natural sites such as ravines, irrigation canals, waterfalls, lakes, high mountain plains, and places where the rainbows appear, for such sites may be inhabited by evil spirits.   (1991: 70)

Of all these dangerous powers residing in the Michacalan environment, we will investigate here only three: evil wind, the mountain spirit and finally *tingu* (confluence).

Evil wind

Certain winds cause a human illness that in Michacala is called 'aerated' (Quichua: *huairashca*). The illness the Michacaleños call *huairashca* is well-known elsewhere in Ecuador (Balladelli, 1990; Estrella, 1977), as well as in other parts of Latin America by the term 'evil wind'. A person gets aerated by a spiritual power which moves along with certain breezes. The wind spirit is invisible, and usually gets linked by Michacaleños only with very cold draughts. According to the villagers, evil wind is the foremost killer of infants,[4] even though adults also may suffer from it and eventually die from its impact.

The symptoms triggered by the evil wind vary widely. They include convulsions, rheumatism, sickness and diarrhoea, fever, stomachache, headaches or chills. As already mentioned, not every chance encounter of Michacaleños with evil wind will necessarily result in the above symptoms. In fact, everything depends on the inner state, or, strength (Quichua: *sinchi*), of the individual at the moment of coming into contact with this negative power. If he or she is tough and courageous (Quichua: *sinchi cana*) usually nothing will happen. But if a person is weak (Quichua: *sampalla*) or frightened (Quichua: *mancharishca*), encounters with evil wind will lead inevitably to even further weakness allowing the symptoms of this illness to take hold. In Michacalan parlance, such a person is taken (Quichua: *japishca*) by the evil wind, i.e. aerated.

In the case of the taboo on new mothers, prohibiting them leaving their houses in the weeks following childbirth, what keeps them indoors is, above all, the fear of such chance encounters with evil wind. Michacaleños argue that women who have just given birth are weak and therefore more prone to falling victim to evil wind. Their weakness from recent childbirth compounded with more weakness by the evil wind could eventually kill them.

To cure evil wind, the sick individual has to pass through a cleansing ritual to drive the malevolent spirit away. The cleansing can be done by any experienced family member, except in very severe cases in which the sick person must seek professional help, for example a specialist in cleansing rituals (Quichua: *pichac*). The parish of Zumbahua has a number of such specialists but an ill person taken by evil wind may even seek the help of a well-known healer (Quichua: *yachac*; Spanish: *curandero*) in a distant town.

Local informants listed a great variety of materials that can be used to cleanse, or sweep (Quichua: *pichana*) a person taken by evil wind. Most prominent among these are liquor, camphor and eau-de-Cologne. In one case we watched a person being swept with herbs by a man who was considered to possess an exceptionally strong virile force (Quichua: *cari cari cana*). It was this force, together with the strong smell of the medicine he used, which was said to be infallible in curing. Other informants advised blowing over (Quichua: *pucuna*) the sick with a mouthful of liquor and tobacco smoke; others advised massages with warm llama fat, or drinking an infusion of various herbs and plants, including coriander (Spanish: *culantro*), herb of grace (Quichua: *ruda*), amapola and carnation (Quichua/Spanish: *runa clavel*).

Michacaleños also know ways to prevent evil wind from taking endangered humans and animals, especially small children. As we will see below, strong odours (Quichua: *asnai*) help keep not only the wind spirit at bay; therefore, small children sometimes carry a necklace and a little ball containing foul-smelling substances.[5]

Taken-by-the-mountain

Another perspective on Michacalan views of the environment is supplied by a human illness called 'taken-by-the-mountain' (Quichua: *urcu japishca*).[6] According to the villagers, typical symptoms of this illness are: an urge to vomit, severe diarrhoea, body aches, paleness and rapid weight loss. In extreme cases, *urcu japishca* can lead to death. Taken-by-the-mountain also accounts for the birth of crippled and deformed babies, premature births, albino children and twins; in other words, *urcu japishca* is responsible for what Michacaleños consider an abnormal or unhealthy new-born. This, logically, links this illness particularly to women, though men may suffer from it as well.

When we started interviewing Michacaleños about the nature of this sickness, it immediately became clear that its name, taken-by-the-mountain, had to be taken seriously. Michacaleños believe that certain, though not all, mountains harbour spiritual beings that can take possession of and sicken a person.[7] Michacala's highest mountains, like the Suni Rumi (Extended Rock), Condor Urcu (Mountain of the Condor), Quitsahua[8] or Turu Rumi (Rock of the Marsh) are all particularly risky in that sense. As it turns out, during the mornings or evenings, these peaks are usually wrapped in thick fog (Quichua: *izhi*) in which the mountain spirit moves about. Therefore, humans should not willingly expose themselves to that fog. Contact with fog inhabited by a mountain spirit, however, does not necessarily or inevitably lead to sickness. A strong individual will indeed withstand any chance encounter with the mountain spirit without any detrimental consequences to his or her health. A person is considered to be strong as long as he or she is physically robust, but also, and more importantly, as long as he or she lives according to the moral standards of personal conduct cherished by the community. Physically weak or fearful as well as anti-social persons, on the other hand, can easily be taken by the mountain. However, some protection against the mountain is always recommended and therefore Michacaleños always take along some liquor when they go to round up semi-wild cattle in the high mountain areas. Cane alcohol provides extra strength and bravery. Considerable courage is indeed called for when Michacaleños circle the semi-wild cattle that range freely over the high *paramos*. Some on horseback, others on foot will round up the herd to drive them down the mountain and into a corral. I certainly often lacked courage when, after a long climb to the mountain top, and clinging to a steep slope, I breathlessly watched the hoof-stamping cattle below ready to defend themselves with their long and sharp horns. I sincerely hoped that it would not occur to any of these animals to break away from the herd and seek refuge in my direction. The fear I felt at these moments is, according to local opinion, very dangerous to health as it is held to soften (Quichua: *sambayachishca*) one's body and soul, making one easy prey for the mountain spirit. Consuming a good quantity of cane liquor addresses the whole issue – as I can confirm.

The concept taken-by-the-mountain is also very interesting in terms of its embedded social and moral theory. We were told that a mountain spirit does not viciously attack a human being. A person must already be weakened to be vulnerable. Above, we mentioned only one of numerous conditions that are considered weakening by Michacaleños: fear or anxiety (Quichua: *manchai*). Further enquiry about the mountain illness revealed that villagers identify many other additional physical and psychological conditions that make a person fall victim to the mountain spirit. Among these are physical debility, egotistical behaviour or attitudes, a solitary lifestyle, and finally, immoral behaviour such as adultery. In other words, the condition of having been taken by the mountain has often decidedly ethical and moral overtones. The sickness is, in fact, often considered a consequence of unethical and immoral behaviour, insofar as such behaviour always weakens the inner state of those who show it, exposing them to the evil influence of malevolent spirits that inhabit the surrounding environment.

According to Michacaleños, children and women are most easily victimized by the mountain. There are essentially two reasons given for this. Children in general are considered frail creatures due to their small size and lack of physical strength. At the same time, they are deemed morally unaccountable. We were told by villagers that it is useless to reproach naughty children because 'they are like little animals and cannot yet reason'. Therefore, nobody blames children for their notoriously self-centred attitudes as their spiritual faculties are still undeveloped. From this, locals conclude that their less-developed physical, social and moral faculties make them more prone to be taken-by-the-mountain. Parents therefore have to watch carefully over small children and avoid exposing them to the dangerous mountains. As they grow up and mature, children will slowly become physically and spiritually stronger at the same time that they transform into truly moral beings.

Like children, women are considered physically weaker than males (as both men and women freely admit). Usually a woman's physical strength suffices to resist the evil influence of wind and mountain spirits. Michacaleños consider females much more prone to fall prey to evil spirits both because of their frequent pregnancies,[9] and because women are thought to be less interested in the general social good. Both males and females defend this idea – surprising to us – by pointing to the fact that women must value the interest of their family more highly than the interest of the community as a whole. Generic interest in the social good is basically seen as a quality of adult males, less developed in females and clearly absent in small children.

Such a conception of age and gender differences does to a certain extent reflect social practice and experience in the village, insofar as men, and only men, spend days on end with other men drinking, chatting and eating together. It is also generally only men who deal with the outside world, either working as migrants in the city or engaging in trade and taking part in village politics. Women, on the other hand, bitterly oppose the tendency of their husbands to spend more time (and money) in general social affairs than with their family. This division in social behaviour then reappears in the male construction of the female gender as being by nature less social.[10]

Michacalan women's continuous complaints about their husbands' over-involvement with other men are simply another side of this ideological construction. From the women's point of view, this over-involvement means they neglect their primary task as providers for their families. During communal work parties, for example, many men regularly get drunk, spending the whole day and often the following one, with their friends in extended social meetings. Any occasion for such drinking bouts is clearly relished by men. Not surprisingly then, unlike Michacalan men, their wives often judge their husbands' involvement in such affairs and, indeed, communal work *per se*, as being of less value than work done in the context of their own family enterprises.[11]

Other criticisms of male behaviour concern their aggressiveness and adultery, both of which Michacalan women consider directly linked to the male habit of leaving their families to attend social gatherings and go on drinking binges. Finally, Michacalan women often complain that their husbands bring too little cash back from their labour migrations, the suspicion being that they spent most of it on themselves in the city with other men (or women). We must remember here that nowadays Michacalan women rely heavily on the cash provided by their husbands in order to maintain their children and the entire household. As mentioned earlier, this cash must cover about half of all family consumption costs. This situation makes women especially dependent on their husbands' income and on the responsible use of the cash they earn during their absence from Michacala.

Significantly, aggression, laziness, the failure to provide for children, but above all marital infidelity are considered activities which soften the culprit's body, thus making him especially receptive to the illness-causing influences of evil wind and mountain spirit. Viewed from this angle, then, it is tempting to see the cultural construction of illness conceptions like evil wind and taken-by-the-mountain as an instrument consciously created and maintained by both Michacalan men and women in their never ending quarrel over their respective social responsibilities, moral obligations and social roles.

For Michacaleños, then, issues of morality are very much at stake in dealing with the mountain spirit and evil wind. This link between a moral lifestyle and good health is also expressed in the Quichua term *alli causai*, which means both good life and health (Hess, 1994). We can quote here two friends who once summarized the moral issues at stake in this way: 'The Michacalan mountains are good. We are the ones with bad thoughts and for this reason the mountain takes us; if we have a good thoughts and a good heart, nothing will happen to us – neither illness nor anything else'.

A person suffering from the mountain sickness must get rid of the bad spirit immediately. This is done as in the case of evil wind by cleansing the body of the sick person, for example, by fumigating it with burning animal bones. Another cure consists of rubbing the sick body with eau-de-Cologne and hot cane alcohol. As with evil wind, the goal is to expel the mountain spirit from the sick person by using the strong odours as remedies.

Tingu

A very dangerous feature to be found in the natural environment are *tingus*. *Tingus* are sites where two (or more) rivers join, pathways cross, crests converge or gorges unite.[12] The term *tingu* is derived from the Quichua term *tinguina* which means to gather, to unite, or to tie something together. Villagers consider *tingus* gathering points for spiritual powers of all sorts, be they the mountain spirit, the souls of dead people (Quichua: *ayacuna*), or the wind spirit. In Michacalan thought, spiritual powers like these do not stray erratically over the landscape, but follow fixed geographical pathways. Where two or more of these pathways join or cross each other, the likelihood of human encounters with these dangerous powers is therefore much stronger. In fact, the uniting of such pathways often provokes what we would like to call a spiritual congestion. Many dangerous spirits, following different paths while wandering over the Michacalan area may join and somehow amass at these points. It follows that lakes fed by many rivulets, gorges that unite valleys, bridges that cross rivers are especially dangerous to humans and their health.

It seems Michacaleños experience their environment subjectively as scattered with potentially dangerous spiritual forces. Some of these powers are stationary, like certain mountain sites, but most of them are highly mobile. They travel with winds and fog along lines and pathways crisscrossing the landscape, accumulating in convergence and crossings, transforming these points into special dangers. Now, this geographical imagery has consequences for the general pattern of physical mobility in this village, that is, for the course of everyday life. Pregnant women, for example, must be especially careful not to encounter the mountain spirit. As already mentioned, women in childbirth refuse to leave their huts for weeks on end. Mothers will make great efforts to protect their babies from evil wind. Youngsters who tend the family herd are warned not to approach 'bad places' or remain idly at crossing pathways. Finally, the selection of house construction sites and pasture areas is based on this local understanding of the Michacalan landscape as internally differentiated in more or less dangerous, healthy or risky areas.

Most interesting, it seems to us, is that the Michacaleños' primary concern with their environment is in relation to human health, since they experience their environment as dotted with locations which are detrimental to their personal well-being. This is even true for the few 'good' places that Michacaleños can point out in their environment. These are places where positive spiritual forces gather. For example, villagers told us about a miraculous waterfall in a neighbouring village which can cure people who suffer from 'bad luck' (Quichua: *chiqui*). Bad luck victims may go to the waterfall and take a shower in its icy water. The locals call this waterfall – not coincidentally – Great Confluence (Quichua: *jatun tingu*).

Conditions for a good harvest

In summing up, we suggest that a scientific and an indigenous understanding of the environmental conditions to crop production and life in Michacala differ markedly. Major differences between both understandings are that for Michacaleños their village soils are suitable for crop production and that it is not the cold climate *per se* that threatens crop yields. Instead, we know that, for Michacaleños, the success or failure of their agricultural activities depends ultimately on divine will. Crop failure and success reflect the will of God the Father, Jesus, and the Virgin Mary as they are the ones that cause crop-destroying or crop-benevolent climatic events to occur. Following on from this view is that the villagers must maintain good relations with these powers in order to avoid their anger and be awarded a good harvest. In Michacala, as elsewhere in the Andes,[13] lack of respect and devotion is thought to lead to subsequent punishment by hail, frost, drought or flood.

It may, of course, be argued that this point is quite trivial, as most people who believe in a supreme being imagine that being to be the ultimate cause of whatever happens to them, and that farmers around the world try to manipulate the divine powers to their own advantage by worshipping them. But this argument should not make us forget the far-reaching practical consequences such convictions imply, especially in relation to questions such as how natural hazards can be acted upon and how it is thought that productivity could be improved.

Michacaleños do not, of course, dispute the fact that frost and hail kill their plants, that plants dry up if it does not rain for a long period of time and that without manure the plants will not grow in Michacalan soils. Still, unlike agricultural professionals, they do not consider their high mountain territory in any way particularly unfit for agriculture. On the contrary, they believe that the basic conditions for agricultural production in their village are quite reasonable.

When asked for their opinions of overall soil quality in Michacala, our informants overwhelmingly declared Michacalan soils to be of 'good to very good' quality for agro-pastoral production (99 per cent of all answers). More than half of the villagers, however, believed that overall productivity had somehow declined during the last couple of decades, while only 38 per cent considered productivity to have remained the same. Finally, only 4 per cent of the interviewees believed that the productivity of Michacalan soils had somewhat increased lately. This result might be taken as an indication of a growing awareness among the villagers of declining soil productivity due to over-exploitation.

But, do Michacaleños causally link declining production to the effects of erosion and the overuse of their soils? Here we argue that this is rarely the case. Only one-fifth of the vast majority of villagers who had complaints about recent declines in soil fertility considered that there had been a decrease in fallow times from four to one to two years, and hence, had realized that over-use of the land was as the cause of declining yields. A majority of Michacaleños (64 per cent of all answers) said plant diseases[14] and an increasing frequency of crop-destroying hail and frost, were responsible for declining productivity. Asked about the ultimate cause of pests and climatic hazards, Michacaleños were unanimous in that these were punishments sent by God (Spanish: *castigos de Dios*), probably in reaction to growing tensions among the villagers. At the moment, only 3 per cent of the village territory is under the hoe, but many Michacaleños are quietly engaged in taking small bites out of the communal *paramo* land to add them to their private fields, causing tensions among community members. Thus, conflicts are increasing as competition for cultivable land increases.

But, how then is a sudden disease or frost explained by the Michacaleños? First, locals differentiate sharply between a normal and an exceptional occurrence. Some worms in a potato field is just how it is meant to be and therefore no reason for particular action. Many worms, on the other hand, is definitely an exceptional state of affairs, that has to be the result of a specific cause. Something must have made the worms accumulate in a particular field. Also climatic events like crop-destroying hail, storm and droughts fall into the category of unnatural events, whenever their consequences threaten the families by destroying the basis of their livelihoods.

Interestingly, Michacalan villagers seem to have quite a selective memory about climatic events. We were long puzzled about our questionnaire data demonstrating the villagers' firm belief that the majority of annual frosts occur during the rainy season.[15] Instead, books on *paramo* ecology and our own temperature measurements indicated that actually, most frosts occur in the dry season. We finally realized that the Michacaleños did indeed notice the numerous frosts during the dry period, but they simply did not care about them because frost in these months does not jeopardize the harvest as most crops are already safely in by then.

So, it is not the *paramo* climate *per se* that seems detrimental to cropping in Michacala. It is only frost and hail that strike when the year's harvest is at stake, which catches the farmers' attention and forces them to seek a causal explanation. In this case, Michacaleños are not at all satisfied with the idea that hail and frost may occur erratically throughout the year. They look for reasons that explain the destruction.

This is of course the same logic that was so brilliantly documented years ago by Evans-Pritchard (1976) with regards to the Azande. His well-known example of the working of that logic among the Azande was a granary whose beams were consumed by termites and collapsed, killing a man. The Azande, Evans-Pritchard explained, knew perfectly well that termites had destroyed the wooden structure of the house, but they still sought an answer to the question: why had the house collapsed precisely at the very moment when that man was resting in its shade? The Azande answer to this question was that this could only be due to witchcraft. In the same way, Michacaleños accepted as perfectly valid that freezing dew destroyed the soft tissue of their crops. But they did not accept this as the whole answer to questions like: Why did the dew freeze last night; and why did it destroy my potato field but my neighbour's?

The belief in divine causation, however, does not mean that the Michacalan villagers are fatalistic about such events. Following their own logic, they attempt to prevent divine punishment, by complying with what they regard as godly demands on their worship.

We had only recently established ourselves in Michacala when we witnessed the following incident. A prolonged drought had seriously delayed the first planting, as the months of October and November had passed without bringing the expected and needed rainfall. Everything had turned bone dry. One morning we overheard a casual conversation among some Michacaleños recalling that farmers of several parish villages had asked the parish priest to say a mass on one of the mountains overlooking Zumbahua. Standing in front of our hut in the village centre, we could see the mountain rising beyond the gorge constituting the village entrance. It is a very steep and cone-shaped one located in the territory of the neighbouring community of Huantopolo. As we later learned, masses had already been read on its peak several times in the past. When the mass was finally held that day on the top of the mountain, many people from the entire parish had attended it, including many Michacaleños. That very same afternoon, the first rain fell, though just a drizzle. To the farmers this was no surprise at all because 'God is pleased by the pious acts of His followers' and an extra mass in the open, on the very top of a mountain, could not help but appease any grudge he might have had with the Zumbahuan people. One of my *compadres* also explained to me that several Michacaleños sponsor regular masses every year to ensure the timely ending of the dry season: 'Rain, gee, when rain is not falling, when the shallots dry up, and the pasture for the animals stops producing, then one has to pray and pledge'.

But, *rogativa*, the word we have translated here as pledge, means more than just praying. It refers to the act of paying for a Sunday mass, putting up candles in the church and trying to appease God with prayers.

But, why is it that Michacaleños so consistently cite God's punishment as retribution for their lack of devotion as the ultimate cause of any climatic event threatening their crops and indeed survival? We can only propose a vague hypothesis that requires further investigation. In a personal communication, the Ecuadorian ethno-historian Segundo Moreno pointed out, that Andean indigenous people seem to have a very different relationship with the Christian pantheon than their Middle American counterparts. He stated that indigenous Mexicans used to consider and treat the Virgin of Guadalupe basically as their benefactor and defender, identifying with her and denying any possibility that she might be willing or able to harm her devotees. Andean people, on the other hand, view the Christian deities and saints with greater ambivalence, seeing them as much as threats to as guardians of their interests.[16]

In a study on Andean religion, MacCormack (1991) notes that when the Spaniards arrived in 1532 the Andean people already viewed their highest deity *Pachacamac* (The Guardian of the World) with that same ambivalence. As she explains, Pachacamac was thought to have created people and to have sustained human beings ever since by making crops grow and curing disease. But, at the same time, he was also considered to have 'brought disease . . . caused earthquakes and the overflowing of the sea' (MacCormack, 1991: 56–7). We find the analogy implied here intriguing, between the Andean deity as described by MacCormack and the present-day Christian equivalent, God, as seen through the eyes of the Zumbahua people. Can it be that present-day Christian concepts have been enfolded within some pre-conquest cognitive scheme?

What is certain is that Michacaleños believe in the need to appease God's bad temper in order to avoid punishments. A common practice in Michacala to preclude divine retribution is to erect straw crosses in the fields immediately after sowing. A villager once explained that 'straw crosses are put up so God may give some crops'. We saw other villagers hacking crosses into the steep mountain slopes right above their plots to give some protection to their plantings.[17] In Michacaleños eyes the very sign of a cross already appeases the Almighty, but, usually stronger measures are called for.

The most elaborate strategy known to Michacaleños to protect their crops from divine punishment is a pilgrimage to certain miraculous shrines. There are several in the Province of Cotopaxi. The one most acclaimed and visited by Zumbahuan people is that of Isinche, some three hours away by bus. But, pilgrimages may also be made to the subtropical town of Baños, or even to faraway Lajas, located in southern Colombia. Most Michacaleños make at least one pilgrimage to the shrine of Isinche with their whole family every other year.

The shrine of Isinche is famous for its image of Jesus as a child, *El Niño*. Isinche is located near Pujilí on the territory of a former hacienda. Other images like the one in Isinche can be found in churches and shrines throughout the highlands, and as we will see, even in some local households. Each *Niño* image is kept and worshipped in a shrine and cared for by his founder (Spanish: *fundador*). In the case of the famous *Niño* of Isinche, the founder built a church with the money donated by believers. This *Niño* is highly prized in the whole of Cotopaxi Province because of its miraculous powers (Naranjo, 1986: 96–102).

Every Sunday, a mass is said in front of huge crowds of farmers and townspeople seeking divine support. The most intense time of veneration of the *Niño* of Isinche, and of others like it, is from Christmas to Epiphany (January 6). I once accompanied a Michacalan family on a pilgrimage to Isinche. We arrived the night before the mass and spent part of the following day with hundreds of other farmers, listening to the mass, praying and entertaining the *Niño* with dances, music and costumes. My companions told me with a happy twinkle in their eyes while putting some candles in front of the *Niño*: 'We put up some candles and pay for the mass, Señorita Carmencita, and therefore the God Father and the God Child, really help us'.

Now, like God, the Isinche Child can become angry, when not venerated as befits it as we learned when we overheard a casual conversation between two Zumbahuan people seated in the back of our project jeep. Their conversation was about the prevailing humid climate, which was seriously threatening the garlic production at the time. One of them mentioned the *Niño* of Isinche, thoughtfully relating the bad condition of the Zumbahuan garlic to the Child: 'The Isinche Child,' she said, 'is truly miraculous but if one does not pay mass in time, it punishes immediately.'

There is a *Niño* in Michacala itself which is considered by the locals to have miraculous properties. Its name is *Niño Mesias* and it belongs to a woman who inherited it from her father. It is said that the *Niño* was found lying on a rock close to where she lives. Once it was taken into the house, the original myth goes, a stranger from a distant village arrived, claiming to be the owner of the image. The *Niño* was grudgingly handed back, only to be soon found again in the very spot where it had been found the first time. In this way it finally became clear to everyone that the *Niño* wanted to stay with the new founder and his or her family.

The owner of the Michacalan *Niño* proudly informed us that she had even built an extra hut just for the image. When we went to see it, it became clear that we were expected to pray and make a pledge and to give a little offering (money, candles) to the *Niño*, to help its founder to care for it. In the *Niño's* hut, there was a painted wooden box in the middle of the room with a small window and a curtain. The *Niño Mesias* rested inside it. Taking a closer look, we saw a thin wooden figure, some 20 cm long with a very oddly worked tiny face. It was wrapped in an old cloth. We were even more surprised when, between the drapes, a second tiny image appeared. The owner of the shrine told us that this was the spouse of the *Niño Mesias* and that she had been given to him by the owner 'to keep Him company'.

Between Christmas and Epiphany each year, families from Michacala and from the neighbouring community of Huantopolo sponsor big festivals for the *Niño*. If in any one year more than one family decides to sponsor a festival, there are still additional dates open for more feasts such as Easter, Corpus Christi or New Year's Day. On any feast day, a mass is held and the *Niño* is carried through the fields and corrals that belong to those that desire his protection.

To sponsor a feast is voluntary in Michacala, based on the need of a family to make a serious pledge for help to the decisive power represented by the image, be it because of some illness or – most probably – to ensure a good harvest. Michacaleños freely admit that they consider the relationship between themselves, on the one hand, and God (represented by the *Niño*) on the other, as one of strict reciprocity: sponsors spend money and other resources to entertain the *Niño* during the religious festival and they expect to receive his help in return.[18]

Michacalan people believe in a direct causal link between their agricultural yields and divine will, although affected by climate or pests. What turns, for example, a frost from an ordinary event into a punishment is God's anger over one's religious conduct. But again we insist that this understanding of ultimate conditions on agricultural production does not make the Michacaleños fatalistic. On the contrary: people continuously manipulate the divine temper by pilgrimages, festivals and the veneration of the *Niño*. In turn, we do suggest that the specific way Michacaleños conceive of the causality behind the natural conditions of existence prevents them from accepting much of developers' talk about how to improve crop yields, because they consider these proposals irrelevant to solving the 'real' problems in cropping.

Up to now, we have concentrated on the distinct ways of conceptualizing the conditions of crop production by academically trained professionals on the one hand and the Michacalan people on the other. The difference in world-view between developers and their indigenous clients highlights the enormous gulf between them. This gap rules out even the possibility of a truly cross-cultural dialogue from the start. The main argument is that speaking across distinct knowledge systems is only possible if developers accept the people's world-view as the basis for proper communication. If developers ignore the local views prevalent among the indigenous people they deal with, they destroy the only basis for legitimate cross-cultural communication and, consequently, for active co-operation with it.

5 Veterinary and indigenous models of sheep management

SINCE THE 1970s, development agencies worldwide have become concerned to promote economic systems that are sustainable in the ecologies they are embedded in.[1] The project, PROFOGAN, was no exception to this trend. From the beginning, PROFOGAN was as interested in the conservation of the *paramos* as an important ecological system as it was in augmenting the *paramo's* productive potential. It was found that the best way to preserve the *paramo* ecology, while still exploiting it economically, is by way of a pastoral economy. Our research focused on studying the inner workings of the agro-pastoral production process in order to suggest changes that would increase its efficiency and output without upsetting the ecology of its host. The belief in the necessity of preserving the ecology of the Ecuadorian natural grasslands (*paramos*) was rooted, above all, in the recognition of the *paramo* function in regulating the water supply in adjacent lower lying eco-zones during the dry season. This role of the *paramo* has recently been jeopardized by two interrelated processes: the tilling of the high mountain grasslands to expand agricultural production and the resulting acceleration of erosion that is its result.

It has to be noted that in its natural state, the *paramo* functions as a kind of sponge. During the rainy season it absorbs great quantities of the torrential equatorial rainfalls, and then continuously releases the stored water to lower elevations during the dry season. The lower areas are badly in need of water throughout the dry period. The sponge function of the *paramo* is based on a specific characteristic of its natural vegetation cover and is maintained only as long as this vegetation cover remains intact.

The *paramo* is covered by bunch and tussock grasses, shrubs, sedges and dense mats of tiny plants that grow near ground level. From an ecological point of view, the most important feature of this vegetation is its complex, deep-root system. As the ecologist Luis Cañadas once explained to us, in the high, humid and frost-plagued *paramos*, the vegetation is characteristically subterranean. The plants mostly grow downwards expanding their root system to the utmost, while the green parts of the plant seek to avoid exposure to the cold climate, pressing themselves against the ground. The extensive root systems of *paramo* plants create a dense capillary web in the top layers of the soil which is capable of taking in and holding in place enormous quantities of rainfall preventing the flooding of lower valley floors during the rainy season. In the dry months, this water is then released in a slow but steady fashion into the diverse river systems of the Ecuadorian highlands that originate in the *paramo* and irrigate the lower elevations. Thus the *paramo* plants' root system provides the indispensable foundation for agricultural production in lower-lying areas. Destroying the *paramo* therefore means putting agricultural production in the central Andean valleys into jeopardy.

The harmful consequences of this accelerated destruction of the *paramo* vegetation cover are already apparent elsewhere in Ecuador. In the Inter-Andean Ambato Valley, for example, tilling and overgrazing have already so severely diminished the absorbing capacity of the *paramos* that the irrigation-dependent lower part of the Ambato valley is now regularly inundated during the rainy season, and nearly barren during most of the dry season. All this happens

51

because most of the annual rainfall received by the upper part of the valley during the rainy season no longer gets absorbed by the spongy soils of untilled *paramos*. Instead, the rain rushes immediately downhill, flooding houses, gardens and fields nearby. During the dry season, on the other hand, the Ambato River receives hardly any water at all, and the ever longer periods of intense drought have already begun to devastate portions of its once intensely cultivated valley floor.

A second example of the catastrophic consequences of *paramo* destruction can be found in the Paute River system in the south of Ecuador. There, tilling of large portions of the surrounding *paramos* has led to an increase in soil erosion. At present, the soil is constantly washed into the river system in enormous quantities. The sediment-laden waters of the Paute then feed into the reservoir of the Paute hydro-electrical project, rapidly filling it up. In 1991, White and Maldonado had pointed out that this process of accelerated sedimentation constitutes a serious threat to the hydro-electric plant's turbines. Between February and March of 1992, their warning suddenly became a reality after a marked delay in the region's annual rainfall. This caused the water-level in the reservoir to fall below a critical point where the amount of sediments present in the remaining water, and circulating through the plant's turbines, increased so much that electricity production became impossible without endangering the machines. The consequence of this was a severe restriction of electricity throughout Ecuador for six full weeks which dealt a heavy blow to the crumbling national economy of the time.

The severe consequences of *paramo* destruction led PROFOGAN to conclude that whatever development strategy was pursued in this eco-zone, the maintenance of the natural vegetation cover had to be one of its central aims.

Since colonial times the *paramo* area in Ecuador has shrunk continuously. Most of the natural grassland has slowly been turned into cultivated fields. Lately, however, erosion of already cultivated portions of this eco-zone has reached alarming proportions as the intensification of land exploitation has been the only remedy for thousands of poor smallholders trying to avoid declining real incomes in the face of their country's galloping inflation.[2] Increased demographic pressure has also recently led to an acceleration of the pace with which *paramo* areas are turned into cultivated fields (Hess 1990).[3] As Dubly (1990) has indicated, only a decade ago the highest elevation for crop production in Ecuador was around 3500 m. Today, this limit has risen to 3900 m, and is set to rise still further in the near future. So to save the *paramo's* original vegetation cover, alternatives to agricultural production in this area are needed more urgently than ever. For ecological as well as economic reasons, expanding crop production without serious soil protection measures is a disastrous choice in *paramo* areas.

With expanded agriculture ruled out for ecological reasons, PROFOGAN decided that the most promising economic alternative for the hundreds of thousands of peasants living at high altitudes was to intensify animal husbandry. Livestock production, however, cannot be indiscriminate in the *paramo*. Again for ecological reasons, the project workers came to believe that a pastoral economy in these high mountains must focus on the breeding of relatively small species, such as llamas, alpacas or sheep. Although sheep are in fact known to be ecologically more destructive than the Andean native breeds, they are nowadays the most important small livestock in the Ecuadorian *paramo*, and it seems unwise for many reasons to try to oppose their predominance. Breeding large livestock such as cattle or horses is clearly more devastating to the natural vegetation cover of the *paramo* so is not a viable alternative. Even in relatively small numbers, overgrazing and trampling by these animals can cause irreversible damage by initiating erosion in steep and humid mountain areas.[4] Andean livestock such as llamas and alpacas, although ecologically preferable, have such a limited market in Ecuador that they do not increase Andean farmers' income.[5]

Faced with the fact that present-day *paramo* populations by and large practise a mixed agro-pastoral economy with a clear emphasis on the economically rational but ecologically unsound crop sector, PROFOGAN's principal aim was to look for ways of strengthening the animal sector in general and sheep breeding in particular in order to increase productive efforts in the ecologically more sound direction. We took as our working hypothesis the fact that indigenous *paramo* residents prefer crop production to animal production, but only because of the clearly greater economic return. Therefore, we thought that to prevent the tendency for continuous shrinking of Ecuador's *paramo* area, animal husbandry had to be made more attractive to the inhabitants of those areas, especially in terms of money.

The project assumed that the kind of animal husbandry that Michacaleños and other *paramo* dwellers have actually practised for centuries is deficient and, at least to a certain extent, responsible for the low economic return that the Michacaleños get from their pastoral sector. We will look at local malpractice and inefficiencies in Michacalan animal management from a scientific point of view. First, however, we want to make it perfectly clear that from our study of the Michacalan case we have come to the conclusion that – contrary to the working hypothesis that informed our involvement with this village – conservation of the Ecuadorian *paramos* which would be ecologically desirable, cannot be expected from any improvement within the existing animal production system alone so long as the national price structure discriminates against the Ecuadorian farmer in the way that it does.

The prevailing price structure in Ecuador keeps the prices for products of the indigenous peasantry deliberately low and the prices for those consumed by them no less deliberately high. This is done by various fiscal means and reflects the urban bias[6] of the ruling élite (Stutzman, 1981: 84). Market prices of basic foods are a highly delicate political matter, and outside the concerns of the project. We concentrated our efforts on the efficiency of the existing systems of animal management in the *paramo*, hoping to identify ways to make this sector financially more attractive so that the *paramo* inhabitants would decide to reduce their involvement in crop production to a minimum.

With this goal in mind, we first had to determine which factors in the existing production system – whether economic, ecological or organizational in nature – most severely limited its overall efficiency and stability. Our approach in this regard, holistic and varied in method, is known as the system approach to farming economies (Brush and Turner, 1987). The essential characteristic of our methodology was to gather in-depth data on the overall agro-pastoral production system. This data collection was designed to enable our project to make integrated suggestions about the necessary changes in certain parts of the system without upsetting other parts of it.[7]

Especially important to our research, for the ecological reasons already mentioned, was the revision of local management practices in livestock. This led us to pursue questions such as: how are the animals tended, fed, cured, sheltered, butchered and sold? Our hope was that by developing extensive knowledge of management techniques, we could identify clues to the system's weakest spots in terms of efficiency. These weaknesses could then be presented to the villagers, discussed and revised with them, and eventually adopted by the farmers themselves.

We had to learn, however, that matters would not work out that easily. In those days we still believed that the basic condition to change was the will of the Michacaleños. We also believed that livestock management was sufficiently technical a matter to be studied and eventually manipulated without too much concern for the overall cognitive system. That is, at least as long as the locals themselves found their current practices wanting and expressed a clear desire to receive technical assistance and advice – which they did. Besides, we thought that management practices in Michacala were probably much better and based on more sophisticated knowledge on the part of the locals than we had ever expected. This opinion was based on previous studies of pastoralists in many parts of the Andean world that emphasize the adaptedness and adequateness of indigenous management practices and belief systems.[8] But in all this, we quickly became disappointed.

In fact, after only a few months in Michacala, we found it quite impossible not to accept as a fact that from the viewpoint of veterinary science,[9] Michacalan sheep are indeed very poorly managed.[10] Emaciated, weak, sometimes crippled, and often filthy, they showed only slow increases in mutton, milk and wool yields throughout their lives. In accord with animal science, a central cause for all this is clearly negligence on the part of the indigenous caretakers, especially with regard to genetic selection, nutrition and healthcare.

Interestingly, most Michacalan villagers fully agreed with our negative analysis of the overall condition of their flocks. They freely admitted that too many of their sheep die, especially the young ones. Their own critical evaluation of local sheep production led them to what we then considered a surprisingly positive attitude toward receiving technical assistance by outsiders in matters of animal husbandry. In fact, an impressive 82 per cent of all Michacalan families showed keen interest in receiving instructions and advice in better livestock management by zoo-technicians and veterinarians from the Ministry of Agriculture. The 18 per cent who did not want advice in these matters explained that this was because they doubted they knew enough Spanish.

Faced with this situation, we repeatedly made the technical advice that Michacalan people demanded accessible to them. But most of these efforts soon led to frustration. The Michacaleños would listen politely to the advice of any animal specialist we were able to bring to the village, but, in the end, they would rarely follow the advice by bringing in the necessary charges.

Why was it that so little of the advice given to the herders at their own request was accepted and integrated into their management practices? We will suggest here that the most significant reason for this is the epistemological and cognitive differences that exist between what we call a veterinary view of sheep husbandry and what can be called the indigenous view. Not surprisingly, Michacalan herders evaluate advice given to them on the basis of their own ethno-theory of how and why animals stay healthy and multiply, or get sick and die. It was on the basis of their own practice and theory that they found much of the advice given to them by the outsiders either simply nonsensical or that they discarded it as impractical without even trying it out.

In order to illustrate the differences between veterinary and local theory and practice, we will present the project and indigenous analyses of the same reality.

We will show that local sheep management rests on an ethno-theory, basically part and parcel of an alternative indigenous world view; a view that shapes Michacalan practices in the same way that the scientific view shapes the advice given by university-trained veterinarians.

Veterinary views of sheep breeding

Sheep science classifies the totality of management practices under a variety of headings, from breeding control and genetic selection to nutrition and health-care. Proper attention to each of these fields will guarantee efficient sheep production and maximum output. This category and classification system implies specific ideas about what type of creature a specific breed of livestock is and how it is related to its environment. More than that, these categories imply not only a particular view of an animal's nature and how it functions, but also a view of how the world the animal inhabits is constituted. In this respect, sheep science, then, implies indeed an embracing world view.

Take for example animal healthcare. The very definition of what falls under the heading of veterinary healthcare implies a particular understanding of what constitutes a healthy or an unhealthy animal. Complex ideas about what causes disease in an animal become in turn the basis of an extensive lore of medicines and curative treatments.

Zoo-technicians and veterinarians habitually compare actual practice in a given location with the model of ideal practice that is dictated to them by university-based education. Whenever actual practice is found to deviate from that education, development experts take the practices observed as clear cases of mismanagement that can and should be replaced by the introduction of the correct practice, if overall efficiency is to be promoted. Following this logic, we dedicated a considerable amount of time and effort to the description and quantification of animal production (including sheep, llamas, pigs and cattle) as actually practised in Michacala, in order to compare that practice with the ideal model of management as defined by veterinary science.

Genetic selection

Within sheep science, the breed of sheep is vital to the overall results of husbandry in terms of mutton, wool and milk. Certain breeds of sheep are better for wool than for mutton, while others are better for milking. Thus, the breed smart farmers acquire should be determined by the kind of sheep products they want. But, of course, not all breeds are equally good for all environments. In Ecuador, the National Association of Sheep Breeders (ANCO) recommends two improved cross-breeds for the Andean highlands: Rambouillet and Corriedale. Both are dual-purpose breeds, that is: equally good for both wool and mutton production. ANCO supports a development programme for poor rural areas that sells relatively cheap, pure-bred rams to the farmers. With these rams, the peasants are then supposed to improve the physical characteristics of their flocks by using them for breeding. But what usually happens is that breeding is not carefully controlled by the peasants, so the favourable characteristics of the pure breeds, such as curlier wool or more mutton per animal, soon tend to disappear.

There are no pure-bred sheep in Michacala. The local breed fall into a category known in Andean countries as *criollo*. A *criollo* is a genetic mix and persists as a distinct type only by constant inbreeding. *Criollos* are relatively poor producers of mutton, wool and milk. They are usually thin, small and their wool lacks curl and density. But, they have one considerable advantage over pedigree breeds like Rambouillet and Corriedale: they are physically more robust and can withstand the adverse climate and poor grazing of the *paramo* grasslands. Our project therefore rejected the introduction of more productive, but less well adapted, varieties in the Michacalan *paramo* as a viable solution to the problem of low productivity. On the contrary, we concluded that only by improving management and health-care for the native *criollos* could herding be made more productive.

Nutrition

According to sheep science, probably the single most important parameter determining the success or failure of sheep breeding is nutrition. In Michacala, sheep rely entirely on the natural grass cover of the village's territory. Therefore, the overall quantity and quality of the village's natural grass cover plays a major role in determining productivity. As a first step towards an analysis of the nutritional conditions of sheep breeding in the Michacalan pastures, we made a botanical inventory. Then we determined the nutritional content of important plant species. This work was done by two zoo-technical graduate students who spent several months setting out this botanical inventory.[11]

Michacalan pastures were divided into three general types: the first one is found in the marshy valley bottoms (Quichua: *turu pampa*). There, cushion and rosette plants predominate.[12] They cover one-fifth of the total village territory. Only a few grasses, usually *Festuca dolicophylla* and *Elymus virginicum,* grow in these wetlands.[13] By far the largest sector of Michacala is covered by a second type of grassland, one the villagers call mother grass (Quichua: *mama ucsha*). This type is dominated by tall (60 to 100 cm) bunch grasses, such as *Calamagrostis sp.*, *Eragrostis purpurensceus*, and *Calamagrostis vinacunarum*. These grasses are fibre-rich but only low to medium in protein content, and they have little appeal to most animals including sheep. Bunch grasses, especially when still green, are preferred by llamas and cattle; sheep clearly prefer the much softer green vegetation which covers the ground below the bunch grasses. Despite their restricted value as fodder, bunch grasses are of great importance for the villagers in many other respects. They are cut and used for fuel and they provide basic material for house and roof construction. In an ecological sense, furthermore, they protect the Michacalan soils against wind and water erosion, especially on steep slopes.

A third, less common type of pasture is found in the rocky sections of steep slopes in all three Michacalan valleys. The vegetation there is generally scarce and relatively unimportant because only goats actually prefer grazing here. Still, these areas are the principal sources of wood to use in the local hearths, for they support some hard-leafed, low-growing bushes like *Chuquiragua insignis* and *Jata* (*Pernettya sp.*).

Zoo-technicians, analysing the adequacy of a natural vegetation cover, like the Michacalan *paramo*, as fodder for sheep, are of course much more interested in the quality of the vegetation cover than in a mere inventory of its plant species. Therefore, a sample of 11 species, considered representative of the total, were sent to a laboratory for a nutritional analysis (Table 4). To simplify the presentation, we reduce the results of that analysis to three important variables: dry matter, proteins and fibre content.

Table 4:   Nutritional value of forage species, in per cent of dry matter

Species	Dry matter	Protein	Fibre
Gramineae			
Calamagrostis sp.	40.64	4.47	41.69
Festuca dolicoph.	46.45	10.72	38.65
Festuca pratensis	40.65	10.97	40.03
Elymus virginicum	25.70	5.37	38.67
Stipa ichu	42.62	6.83	37.77
Aristida longespica	47.45	5.78	35.74
Leguminae			
Vicia graminae	32.40	24.14	31.72
Compositae			
Baccharis servillifolia	41.86	6.03	31.87
Lucilia aretioid.	24.69	5.03	21.25
Werneria nubigena	25.60	6.22	25.09
Rosaceae			
Alchemilla orbiculata	24.22	15.15	18.88

Source 8

The data reveal that all Gramineae involved are low to mediocre in nutritive quality compared to improved forage, especially in terms of protein content; but with very high fibre content. As already indicated, it is this type of relatively poor forage that predominates in the natural pastures of Michacala. Unfortunately, protein-rich forage like *Astragalus pattersoni* and *Vicia gramineae* cover less than 2 per cent of the total pasture land of the village. Legumes are more frequent in the humid valleys than on the grassy slopes. This means that the overwhelming majority of the natural grass cover in the community has little appeal to most grazing animals, especially sheep.

As already mentioned, sheep prefer the green and soft ground-level growth found among the bunch grasses and on valley bottoms. In Michacala these are Compositae and Rosaceae that like to grow in wet flats. Among these, *Alchemilla orbiculata* is clearly predominant. It has relatively high protein content and abundant fibre, too. Unfortunately, the wet grounds on which this species grows are also the preferred breeding ground for most sheep parasites in Michacala, among them liver flukes (*Fasciola hepatica*), lung worms, and round-worms. These parasites contribute to the high mortality rates in sheep.

As discussed in Chapter 2, Michacalan soils are deficient in phosphorus, which causes generally poor plant growth but also leads to phosphorus deficiency in the forage growing on that soil. That deficiency becomes even more aggravated during the dry season, when most plant parts dry up. Sheep tended on phosphorus-deficient pasture grow much slower than normal. They have higher feed requirements, poor appetite, turn listless and often develop deformations of their extremities (knock-knees). *Aphosphorosic* ewes give birth to weak lambs and produce little milk (Ensminger, 1970: 218).

All these symptoms are indeed common in Michacalan flocks. These problems could easily be solved by feeding the sheep salt enriched with minerals. Such a supplement would easily improve the physical well-being and production of sheep. Unfortunately, up to now, salt has never been given to any sheep in Michacala. Not only do the villagers consider salt feeding far too expensive, they also consider it superfluous. Only ewes which have recently lambed are given some better quality forage. They are put on a parcel of lush pasture which is often available in onion gardens. In these gardens, ewes and lambs do not have to move around to find forage, which saves energy. However, although this behaviour is appropriate, only very few animals benefit from it, and mostly for periods grossly insufficient for substantially strengthening the weakened ewes. To resume, it can be said that – even though extensive – Michacalan *paramos* are quite poor feeding grounds for sheep production. In fact, it is only the importance of these *paramo* grasslands which prevents agro-scientists from recommending the replacement of its natural grass cover with improved forage as the first basic step in improving animal husbandry.

Management practices

The term management stands for a great variety of practices that are applied to sheep to improve their physical well-being and hence boost mutton, wool, meat and milk yield. We will discuss sheltering, tupping, castrating, docking, post-natal care, shearing, milking and manure collection to give a picture of sheep management in Michacala. There are many other practices applied in commercial and scientific sheep raising, such as early weaning of lambs, hoof trimming and cutting horns, but these are not customary in Michacala. Their lack is in itself evidence of sub-optimal handling of sheep, if judged from a technical point of view.

Sheltering

Sheep spend the night in corrals close to the home of their owners. There are several types of corrals in use within the village. The majority of enclosures are made up of dirt walls and wooden barriers. One-fifth of all corrals are entirely made of wood, even though these offer no protection whatsoever against the icy winds and storms of this high-mountain region. Some corrals are dug into the ground or are entirely made up of earthen walls. These, of course, offer more protection against the harsh, cold climate in Michacala, but only 20 per cent of Michacalan family herds have the luck to sleep nights in one of these.

Tupping

Strict control of breeding is the principal means of maintaining or improving the quality of a herd. But in Michacala, this form of control is exercised by only seven per cent of the flock owners, and even they try to control tupping in only a few of their animals. Controlling the mating behaviour within a herd is particularly difficult in Michacala, as male and female sheep are customarily tended together and are housed in the same corrals at night. To control breeding effectively, Michacaleños would therefore have to make significant changes to their present herding practices, starting with the permanent separation of male and female animals in distinct herds. This would only make sense, of course, if various smaller family herds were actually pooled into one, which could then be split up again into male and female flocks. Such a change in sheep management would have several advantages. Genetic reproduction could become a real option; and larger flocks would make it worthwhile to put experienced adult shepherds or shepherdesses in charge of them instead of leaving them tended by small children, as often happens nowadays. The presence of more experienced shepherds would likely increase the security of the animals during grazing, and reduce losses due to accidents or predators.

From a zoo-technical point of view, Michacaleños are also negligent concerning control of first lambing of their ewes. An undesirable consequence of uncontrolled inter-breeding within Michacalan herds is that most village sheep are impregnated very young, often immediately on reaching sexual maturity. In Michacala, the average age of ewes at first lambing is only 21 months. This means that the female is fertilized when only 16 months old. Premature pregnancies have several harmful consequences among Michacalan sheep. They cause physical weakness and subsequent poor physical development in the ewe as well as in her lambs. They may also explain the unusually long period between lamb births observed in Michacalan sheep. We found the average period between births to be 317 days, much longer than in healthy sheep elsewhere. A third and related consequence of premature motherhood in Michacalan sheep is probably a marked retardation of post-natal fertility in the ewe. Michacalan dams need an average of some 167 days to become fertile again after parturition. As a result, a considerable portion of the adult female sheep in the village reproduce only every other year.

Castration
Castration of rams is another method of controlling the quality of one's herd. Unfortunately, in Michacala, castration is hardly ever used to exclude rams with unfavourable physical characteristics like deformations. If Michacalan herders castrate at all, it is done either to calm down particularly restless animals, which make herding difficult, or to fatten animals faster. Few sheep owners actually castrate sheep. Two out of three, in fact, maintained that they had never done it before.

The Michacaleños' method of castration differs quite radically from those recommended by veterinary science. Villagers castrate rams when they are 14 to 18 months old, an age considered by zoo-technicians to be far too late. The scientifically recommended age for castrating is before the lamb is even three weeks old. Late castration is thought to cause the animal much more stress and is accompanied by a much higher risk of infection. Furthermore, Michacaleños castrate without any hygienic precautions: any knife, often a blunt and dusty one, may be used. The person who does the castrating is usually experienced and thus in some sense a kind of indigenous veterinarian, called in Quichua *huihua yachac*, meaning literally, he who knows about animals. Yet it is not customary for the castrator to wash his hands before the operation or treat the wound with a disinfectant. Instead after the extraction of the testicles some even apply vegetable or pork fat to the fresh wound, which – according to a veterinarian consulted on that matter – has no curative effect at all.

Docking
Michacaleños practise docking – the removal of the tail of a lamb – much more often than they do castration. In fact a majority of sheep owners customarily dock at least some of their animals. The principal reason given for this practice by zoo-technicians is to facilitate the impregnation of the animal. A secondary reason to dock is to improve the sanitary condition of the sheep, as otherwise dung gets caught in its tail. In Michacala, however, female and male animals are sometimes docked. Michacaleños dock when the animal is already about 16

months old, or nearly adult. Sheep specialists, on the contrary, recommend docking during the first two weeks of a lamb's life in order to keep blood loss and stress during the operation to a minimum. Moreover, it is common to see docked animals in Michacala whose tails are not cut close enough to the britch area to significantly facilitate impregnation.

Post-natal care
A further inadequacy in Michacalan sheep management is that insufficient attention is given to the new-born lambs. A third of the families interviewed admitted to looking after new-born lambs only to assure their protection against the cold at night. Another reason given to care for the new-born is to protect it against predators, especially if it is born in the *paramo* during grazing time. Nevertheless, the vast majority of sheep owners pay no attention to neonates whatsoever. Many of our informants on this point argued that they cannot know when the ewe will give birth and thus cannot know when to be nearby. Some even giggled at the idea of helping a lamb or ewe during the process of birth or shortly afterwards, as they believe that the animals know best how to do it in this situation. Others argued that any human intervention would only frighten the ewe to death.[14] Post-natal care, such as disinfecting the navel of the new-born with iodine, is not practised and is indeed considered superfluous by the villagers. Considering the lack of protection given to new-born lambs, both against the freezing night temperatures and against navel infections, it should come as no surprise that mortality in neonates is very high in Michacalan sheep herds.

Shearing
Wool is a very valuable sheep product in Michacala. It is used to weave ponchos which are worn by all men, belts (Quichua: *chumbicuna*) and shoulder cloths (Quichua: *bayeta*) for the women. But, shearing in Michacala is often badly timed and done without any hygienic precautions. The first shearing of a sheep is done when it is some 14 months old. This first cut is considered of inferior quality by the villagers because the fleece is still too fragile for spinning. It attracts a much lower market price than the wool of adult animals. From that time on, the animal is sheared every year. Most animals are sheared during the dry season. But many herders in Michacala believe that shearing is possible throughout the year, with the only exceptions being those periods with the heaviest rainfalls, such as March and April.

For shearing, the sheep is thrown down wherever it is caught. Its legs are bound together. First, with the animal lying on its right side, the shearer, who is usually the male head of the family, starts cutting from the stomach area upwards to the back. Next he cuts from the head down the neck and throat and then down to the shoulders. Then the animal is turned on to its left side and the shearer begins cutting from the belly up to the back again. Finally, the wool from the lowest belly area is cut. A shearing by an experienced Michacaleño takes some 25 minutes.

Usually, lots of keds, in Spanish known as *garrapata* (*Melophagus ovinus*), appear in the clip. Shearing would of course be the best time and opportunity for treating infested animals with anti-parasitic sprays or liquids. But in practice only one-third of the villagers treat their sheep for this pest at all, and most of them do so by applying a generic insecticide – or strangely enough –a disinfectant or even kerosene. Those who do so, do it whenever they consider it necessary – which is not always after shearing.

Milking and meat production

Another important sheep product in Michacala is milk. A good milk ewe will give some 100 ml each day during the first month or two after parturition. After that period, daily milking of ewes slows down to as little as 20 ml per animal. This reduction in the quantity of milk taken, as well as the villagers' deliberate selection of only the better milk ewes for milking shows the villagers' concern for their lambs; yet when seen from the perspective of the generally emaciated lambs, any extraction of milk lowers their chances of survival, and does not seem to be at all advisable under the environmental circumstances in Michacala.

Meat production in Michacala is also of low efficiency. In three family herds, for example, we weighed all the sheep. The adult sheep were not very heavy, averaging only some 49 kg, less than half the average weight of a North American sheep. The total range from lightest to heaviest animals was 38 to 60 kg. This is another result of sub-optimal sheep nutrition in Michacala. Young animals were found to gain weight very slowly, and most were sold only when they were at least four years old, by which time their teeth had been badly ground down from chewing the hard *paramo* forage.

Manure collection

The most important product of sheep husbandry in this village is dung (Quichua: *huanu*). As we have already said, without it, agricultural activity would rapidly become impossible in this eco-zone.[15] Manure is collected from the corrals only on dry days. Michacalan women and children gather an average of 133 sacks of dung per year from their small herds of sheep, llamas and goats. This might seem an impressive harvest from a family herd of llamas plus sheep of no more than 31 head on the average. Unfortunately, to fertilize just one hectare of potatoes, 183 sacks of dung are used in Michacala, or more than the family actually has.

In the light of these facts, the current method of collecting dung shows serious deficiencies. Corrals are swept only every four days during the dry period. As Michacaleños do not use any bedding for their sheep, large amounts of dung are lost through run-off dissolved in the urine of the animals. Even more dung is lost during rainy periods. Such losses could be avoided with the provision of some dry grass bedding and a roof. Any loss of dung is extremely unfortunate in an economy which needs large quantities of manure to produce tubers. Indeed, one-fifth of all families in Michacala declared that they lacked enough manure for their tuber fields in any given year. The alternative of using chemical fertilizer is not feasible for Michacaleños because of the overly high price of fertilizers in the national market in comparison with average family income in this village; as already indicated in Chapter 2.

Sheep health

A major management issue for any zoo-technician is, obviously animal healthcare. In Michacala, as in all *paramo* communities, sheep are plagued by a great variety of diseases, which – from the technical point of view – seems a logical result of poor feeding and bad management. Proper healthcare is therefore a critical feature of any attempt to improve the economic profitability of the livestock sector in *paramo* economies.

One clear sign of severe health problems in a flock is the presence of crippled animals, which are rather common in Michacala. Coughing and sneezing sheep are also common. Some of these animals may actually develop severe lung diseases. Cases of arthritis have been observed too. Animals suffering from this disease show swollen leg joints and have a hard time getting on their feet. We were also told about a severe epidemic that killed many animals in this village only a couple of years ago. Most likely it was an outbreak of foot-and-mouth disease. In what follows, we will concentrate on only the most common diseases in Michacalan flocks. These are chronic eye infections, external parasites, diarrhoeas and intestinal disorders (Table 5 below).

Eye infections
In a random sample covering 20 per cent of the sheep-owning households in Michacala, all the illnesses that had affected the households' flocks during a previous two-year period were identified. The villagers completed a questionnaire and their flocks were examined. The most frequent disease hitting Michacalan sheep was a chronic eye infection, or *conjunctivitis*. This disease is easy to detect, as the infected animal's eyes are covered with a yellow-white coloured scum. The infection severely impedes the animal's vision, which is more prone to accidents than a healthy animal, especially when grazing on the rugged terrain of the upper *paramo* range.

External parasites
The second most frequent ailment in sheep was found to be external parasites, especially so-called *garrapatas*. These are wingless flies that are up to one-third of an inch long and live off sheep blood. Heavy infestation with these parasites, as is so often the case in Michacalan sheep, leads to severe anaemia and emaciation, and may even damage the wool fleece. Indeed, ticks, in combination with some other disorder, may well kill an animal, particularly if they infest an already weak animal.

Intestinal disorders
Diarrhoea is a frequent occurrence in Michacalan flocks. We were differentiating two basic forms of this illness: a diarrhoea due to intestinal inflammations (*Enteritis*) and one due to internal parasites. The first one is identifiable by phlegm in the sheep's faeces, while parasitic diarrhoea can be identified by the presence of blood in the faeces. At a later stage of the study, we also collected droppings from three randomly selected flocks. Laboratory examination of these samples revealed a massive infestation of Michacalan flocks with internal parasites, such as round worms, of which two varieties predominated: *Nematodirus* and *Trichostrongylus*. Surprisingly, the lab test did not confirm our suspicion about the presence of liver flukes, known as *Fasciola hepatica*.

Intestinal disorders are indeed very common in Michacalan sheep. However, none of them is necessarily fatal if treated at an early stage. If the animals are not treated adequately, though, these illnesses can lower the physical resistance to such a level that even minor additional complications may kill an animal. The first animals to fall prey to these diseases are of course the physically weak ones, such as new-born and malnourished sheep.

Treatments
How do Michacalan sheep owners try to cope with the multiple ailments that plague their animals? Table 5 documents not only how frequently the already mentioned illnesses affect sheep in this village, but also how few of the flock owners actually trouble themselves to treat their animals at all. The percentages

Table 5: Sheep illnesses, treatments and efficiency

Illness	Affected flocks (%)	Sheep owners who treat (%)	Treatment efficacy
Eye infection	93	100	high
Hoof-rot	67	83	high
Enteritis	81	73	low
Internal parasites	44	46	low
External parasites	89	33	high

Source 7

given in the third column of Table 5 illustrate different degrees of care given by herd owners, ranging from quite good to far too little, according to a PROFOGAN veterinarian. For example, while eye infections are treated by all the herders, other illnesses receive attention only by some of them. A high degree of curative negligence relates to internal parasite infestations and keds. A majority of the sheep owners does not even try to treat these plagues. From a zoo-technical point of view, the overall curative behaviour among Michacalan sheep owners shows serious shortcomings.

The fourth column in Table 5 shows the villagers' own opinions about the effectiveness of the known cures. As can easily be seen, most informants indicated that they considered the cures known to them in the case of eye infections, hoof-rot and keds to be highly effective, while they considered those cures known to them in the case of enteritis and intestinal parasites to be of very low efficacy.

The above findings triggered another phase of research in which we tried to find out about medicines given to sick animals in Michacala. Once we established a list of the most frequently used remedies and treatments for all of the classified sicknesses, we then consulted a PROFOGAN veterinarian[16] concerning the appropriateness of the remedies named by the villagers and his evaluation of the effectiveness of treatments as given in the community.

Michacaleños know an impressive array of remedies against eye infections in sheep (Quichua: *nahui uncui*). Some villagers recommended dissolving medicine containing penicillin in the urine of a llama or a baby and then washing the eyes of the sick animals with that solution. Others preferred to apply Terramicina and Sulfotierol, which are both antibiotics recommended by vets. Most villagers still preferred to treat *nahui uncui* with lukewarm water in which salt or an antacid stomach reliever like *Alka-seltzer* or *Sal Andrews* was dissolved. The encrusted eyes were then washed with this solution. Still other informants indicated that in order to cure the eye sickness, milk from a nursing woman or llama urine should be used. A further group cured the ailment with juice squeezed out of a pasture plant, known in Spanish as *orejuela* (*Alchemilla orbiculata*) and in Quichua as *chisic*. It would be interesting to research this plant, as villagers also use it in a masticated form for curing tooth infections and skin contusions.

For curing hoof-rot, or as Michacaleños more accurately call it, split foot (Quichua: *chaqui chicta*), some villagers admitted using veterinary disinfectants such as Yodo Salil and Eterol. Others mentioned the use of hydrogen peroxide. The veterinarian considered all three of these remedies sound. Other cures practised in the community consisted of applying lemon juice or sugar-cane alcohol to the infected feet. The veterinarian thought that these remedies could not conceivably be effective, but probably can alleviate the ailment somewhat.

This is also true in the case of a massage with lard, which some Michacaleños do to infected animals' hooves. These massages probably relieve the pain and soothe the rotting skin, but they cannot cure the infection. Although the veterinarian had mixed opinions about the effectiveness of the mentioned remedies, the villagers judged them all, without exception, to be highly effective.

The generic term for diarrhoea in Quichua is *quicha*. Michacala's sheep owners recognize different types of diarrhoea – as, for example, those with or without blood or phlegm in the droppings. Some herders said they bought veterinary antibiotics such as Agromicina to cure diarrhoea in their animals. From a veterinary point of view this is indeed the best way to kill internal parasites. A majority of herders, however, used only a mixture of water and lemon juice, or a solution of bicarbonate which they then force fed the animals.

According to the veterinarian, these remedies may calm intestinal inflammations, which are often provoked by parasitosis, but they will not kill the internal parasites. The same is true for some other infusions used in the village, of eucalyptus leaves and camomile and the fibre of a fresh corn cob.[17] Finally, some villagers even give their sheep affected by diarrhoea a shot of sugar-cane alcohol mixed with sulphur. One woman told me that her family used a variety of herbs and plants that grow in subtropical areas, such as *Hondovalle*, and local plants, such as *Santa Maria* (Feverfew) and *Allcu micuna milin* (*Bromus catarticus*) to treat parasites. As she explained, one must make a bedding for the sick sheep and allow them to pass several nights on the bedding as a cure. The veterinarian could not imagine how these plants could actually cure parasitosis through mere contact.

Ticks called *garrapatas* in Michacala are a most common pest in sheep. We have seen men and women picking literally hundreds of them from the fleece of an infested sheep shortly after shearing. The villagers separate the keds' heads from their bodies to ensure the death of these extraordinarily pressure-resistant insects. In order to control the pest, most villagers recommended insecticides in the form of sprays and liquids. Some used Negubon; others, in fact a majority, preferred the much more poisonous Baygon and even DDT. Even though all these products are indeed effective in killing the ticks, they are clearly not recommendable as medicine, because of their toxicity to animals and humans alike. Finally, some Michacaleños rubbed their infested animals with kerosene or Cresso – a simple disinfectant. Both methods were considered by the veterinarian to be of doubtful efficacy. What is most surprising of all, though, is that most villagers did not even attempt to cure their flocks with any of the above-mentioned remedies.

A critical review

So far in this chapter, we showed that Michacalan sheep owners manage their animals quite badly by veterinary standards. Take, for example, the practice of docking. Though quite a number of villagers dock their animals, they dock only a few animals and not all the eligible ones. Remember also that docking female sheep is supposed to facilitate mating and keep the britch area clean. But Michacalan docking practice seems not to be motivated by those aims at all, as villagers dock even male sheep, or dock only the tip of the long tail in female animals. Finally, against all zoo-technical recommendation, Michacaleños dock the animals when they are already grown up, but refuse to do so while they are still young.

Another case which raises doubts about the adequacy of local knowledge is castration. As mentioned earlier, in Michacala castration is most often done to calm a troublesome, aggressive animal and only infrequently as a breeding or population-control measure. For castration to become an effective breeding measure, rams logically must be castrated before they reach maturity. But again, Michacaleños never castrate until the animal is adult.

Moreover, Michacaleños follow such seemingly strange rules as those which demand that docking and castration be done during a new moon to prevent 'cold' from getting into the animal's body through the wound in its scrotum.[18] Michacaleños possess similar notions about other bodily openings such as wounds or the navels of new-born animals, which are considered a particular health danger because they may allow penetration of the body by a cold agent; in this case moonshine, but in other cases an evil wind. Inner putrefaction and flatulence are, to the Michacaleños, typical signs of a cold illness affecting an animal. Villagers massage the wound carefully with pork fat after the operation to keep 'cold' from penetrating the animal's body. As one of my *compadres* explained: cold makes the body rot inside and inflates the poor animal which must inevitably die.

What are we to make of all this? Can it really be that Michacalan shepherds, whose ancestors have been shepherds for centuries, have no idea how to handle their livestock with greater competence? Do they really perform practices like docking in the manner they do because their ancestors may have learned them as serfs during *hacienda* times, even though they never really understood how to apply them accurately? Can it be that they are following curative customs despite their obvious ineffectiveness?

Researchers who have taken up such questions in other geographical contexts have given numerous explanations. Some have argued that rural people like the shepherds of Michacala simply lack viable alternatives to their own practices, whether because some supposedly superior alternatives do not actually work or because those alternatives are unaffordable in a specific socio-historical setting. Others have argued that many of the indigenous curative practices have been proven empirically to be accurate, often even superior to western ones (Hughes, 1968). Nevertheless, in the case of Michacala, we feel that these explanations of peasant behaviour remain incomplete.

In reinterpreting the allegedly deficient sheep management encountered in Michacala, several recent studies by the anthropologist McCorkle have proven to be particularly helpful to us. In a very similar context to ours, this author has studied animal production in an indigenous agro-pastoral context in the highlands of Peru (McCorkle, 1982, 1983, 1989, 1992). Like us, she was working in the context of a research and development project with particular interest in livestock production, which is why similarities between our work and her own abound.

In her study, McCorkle too found local animal management and healthcare practices deficient when judged from the perspective of formal veterinary science. But, unlike us, she tries to explain the inadequacies of local knowledge and practice basically by pointing out two aspects of Andean agro-pastoral economies in general: first, the severe constraint on the time available to agro-pastoralists in the overall context of their Andean productive systems, and second, the alien origin of sheep in the Andes.

In fact, the peasants studied by McCorkle undoubtedly lacked time for more intensive sheep care, because of their mixed economy. Besides sheep, these farmers produced a large variety of crops in a very ample territory throughout the entire year by highly labour intensive and very time-consuming technologies. Sheep management, McCorkle therefore concludes, is simply that part of their overall production system that suffers most from the peasants' time constraints, because of its secondary importance within the system (e.g. 1983 and 1992).

The second argument brought forward by McCorkle in order to explain the bad physical condition of sheep flocks encountered in her study (especially as compared with llamas), is that sheep are an alien breed in the Andes, being in fact of Old World origin.

Contrary to sheep, llamas are a domesticate of Andean origin, derived from a wild ancestor already well adapted to the specific demands of this high-mountain habitat. Sheep, on the other hand, are in fact a fairly recent import into the high Andes in evolutionary terms and therefore less adapted to the particular ecology. A related argument here is that native Andean people have had less time to accumulate knowledge about sheep, which might explain why their handling of native llamas is superior. But how much time is necessary to accumulate adequate practical knowledge? And: does such adequate knowledge really always have to be invented independently? At least in the case of Michacala, the region's history suggests that locals have had sufficient time to accumulate certain technical knowledge about sheep breeding transferred to them by the hacienda regime.

The Michacaleños have lived for nearly three and a half centuries within an area, dedicated nearly exclusively to the production of sheep and cattle. Admittedly non-local overseers of the *hacienda* of Michacala and the neighbouring one of Zumbahua, might well have taught the Michacaleños to dock, castrate and salt-feed hacienda animals without ever explaining to them the reasons behind them. But 350 years is a long time for finding this out somehow, as these management practices were applied to the hacienda's animals quite systematically until the 1950s, and very much with profit-maximizing goals in mind.[19]

However, even though these practices had to be applied to the *hacienda's* animals adequately, the Michacaleños never adopted those practices, or adopted them only incompletely, for the management of their own flocks. More than that: even when our project experts did explain to the Michacaleños how to apply those techniques – and why – most villagers listen attentively, but seemingly forgot most of the advice anyway.

It was only after many such frustrating experiences that we finally came to the conclusion that the main problem with our project's intentions to improve animal management was that we were completely unable to put across to local people why they should try the alternative practices we proposed, as the reasons we pointed out obviously were not persuasive for them.

When that conclusion finally dawned on us, we remembered the patient yet doubting looks on the faces of the Michacaleños whenever we tried to explain the vicissitudes of intestinal parasites or of epidemics. We suddenly came to see that the very way we had argued our case, judged from a Michacalan viewpoint, had always been to the villagers the strongest argument against whatever we had said. For the very incomprehensibility of arguments had obviously constituted a clear proof to them that we had not even understood the very basics of the troubles that – in their view – plagued their herds. With that idea in mind, we then decided that a completely different approach was needed, and that we had to try to gain access to the Michacalan views and explanatory theories about animals, health, diseases and cures to really understand the animal management practices we were observing among them.

The enquiry into local etiologies of animal as well as human disease, triggered by that conclusion, became a time-consuming endeavour. But, as a result, we believe that we finally achieved a fair understanding of local sheep management practices and theories of animal illness. In trying to clarify local veterinary knowledge we have, indeed, found it particularly useful to investigate indigenous conceptions of human and animal illness together, as according to the Michacaleños, the logic and theories of causality in both cases are quite similar – just as they are in human medical and veterinary sciences as has been argued elsewhere (McCorkle, 1989). The true test of our approach is of course whether it is capable of explaining the practices of Michacalan herders which a scientific, veterinary approach would only qualify as inadequate. This will be the guiding issue of the following sections.

An indigenous model of sheep health

The principal limit of our questionnaire concerning sheep management and healthcare in Michacala was that it was set up according to scientific descriptive illness categories. This made us blind to the underlying etiological conceptions held by the Michacalan people themselves. We committed the same mistake Howes (1980: 342) criticized in a paper on development and indigenous knowledge; namely that 'Questionnaires impose the compiler's categories upon the respondent and do violence to the latter's meaning system.' Though, on a purely descriptive level, formal-veterinary and local knowledge turned out to be easily comparable, a mere similarity of descriptions of symptoms does not, of course, imply a similarity in causal explanations of the illnesses identified by veterinarians and locals. Zoo-technicians and indigenous informants, for example, both identified hoof-rot as a most virulent health problem among sheep. According to veterinary knowledge, hoof-rot is an infection promoted by overly long exposure to dirty, wet and marshy pasture areas and corrals. The villagers confirmed that hoof-rot appears mostly during the rainy season. Still the local explanation of hoof-rot bears no similarity at all to an infectious disease theory.

Instead local explanations of hoof-rot in Michacala relate it to the evil influence of *rainbow*. This notion, together with three other concepts, locally identified as 'bad luck', 'sinister person' and 'witchcraft', constitute the heart of what we have come to call a Michacalan model of sheep management. In what follows, we will analyse these four illness concepts which will help us to make sense of animal healthcare practices in Michacala. As we will show, the local theory explains most forms of cures and animal handling observable in Michacala, even those that – if judged from a veterinary perspective alone – make no sense at all, or could be considered harmful. Michacalan theory that we are going to outline on the next pages, provides a surprisingly accurate explanation of actual peasant behaviour, especially if compared with the scientific veterinary one.

Rainbow

The first illness concept we will discuss here is 'rainbow', in Quichua known as *cuichi*. In other parts of Ecuador, 'rainbow' is more commonly known as a cause of illness only in humans.[20] In Michacala, rainbow is a cause of illness and death only in animals, and most commonly in sheep.

Rainbows occur frequently in *paramo* areas during the rainy season, when drizzle often coincides with the first sunbeams. Michacaleños believe that those areas where a rainbow touches the ground somehow become contaminated, and that all animals foraging in such areas will necessarily fall ill.

Also, water sources such as rivers and puddles whose waters are murky, multi-coloured or of an oily appearance are locally believed to have been touched by the rainbow. Therefore such water sources are called in Quichua *cuichi yacu*, that is rainbow water. As we already mentioned in Chapter 4, many puddles in the humid pampas of Michacala are multicoloured and, besides that, many village creeks possess a red-yellow-greenish colour because of dissolved sulphur oxides.

The illness resulting from drinking here or even touching such water is called locally 'taken-by-the-rainbow', in Quichua *cuichi japishca*.[21] Sheep are the most likely victims of the rainbow sickness. Whenever affected, they show symptoms such as hoof-rot, weight loss, infestation with keds, intestinal worms and swollen bellies (Quichua: *huicsa ismuchicrishca*).[22] Villagers know, of course, about certain internal parasites, especially worms, as they are often found in the internal organs of slaughtered animals. But for Michacaleños, intestinal parasites of any kind clearly are not a part of the natural order of things. Their presence in an animal requires specific explanation. 'Rainbow' is such an explanation in local people's eyes. Rainbow can also make ewes less fertile or even sterile in some cases. Some villagers explained that when taken by rainbow, the legs of the afflicted sheep will soon become stiff. It will therefore be unable to get on its feet and will die within a week. Michacaleños believe that the rainbow is the principal cause of death in their lambs and hence the most serious natural enemy of their herds.

Treatment
As the affliction by rainbow is, from the Michacalan point of view, caused by a spirit getting hold of the animal, healing must expel the illness-causing spirit. This is done through a cleansing ritual.[23] Sick sheep, and sometimes even entire flocks, are led on to a certain trail, into a gorge or sometimes to a spot close to a river to be cleansed. This is necessary as the villagers believe that the rainbow spirit, after evacuating the animal, will only travel away from their village if it is allowed to follow a river, ditch, trail or some gradient that naturally leads beyond the village borders.

In preparation for cleansing, the shepherd gathers certain brushes and herbs in the surrounding *paramo* and buys some subtropical plants in a coastal market that are indispensable if the ritual is to be effective. We were given the following list of plants that might be used in the cleansing procedure: Chilca (*Baccharis polyantha*), Quishuar (*Buddlei incana*), Eucalyptus (Spanish: *eucalipto*), Worm-wood (Spanish: *ajenjo*), peppermint, *Tetera* and *Hondovalle*.[24] All these plants are tied into a bundle with which the sick animal is then beaten until all the leaves have fallen off. In this way, the evil power that afflicted the animal is said to be chased away.[25] While doing all this, the herder will repeatedly shout, '*Cuichi llucchi. Cuichi llucchi. Urami ri*' (that is: 'Leave rainbow! Retreat rainbow! Go away and down').

As already stated above, hoof-rot is probably the most frequent affliction caused by rainbow in Michacala, although this affliction is also sometimes thought to be caused by 'bad luck' or even 'witchcraft'. With this information in mind, some of our informants' strange answers as to what can be done to cure hoof-rot make perfect sense. We were told, for example, by many Michacaleños that iodine, a disinfectant or even hydrogen peroxide are effective remedies in the case of hoof-rot. According to our project veterinarian, these substances may have soothing effects, but, from the villagers' point of view, they are in fact stinky substances and, their malodorous quality enables them to drive away the evil rainbow power that is the ultimate cause of this affliction in Michacalan eyes.

Explaining the choice of substances used in curing rituals in Michacala by reference to their odorous qualities (or sometimes their thermic qualities, as we will describe later) does indeed make some sense of nearly all the remedies and treatments used by the villagers. For example, we were told of a cure of an acute outbreak of rainbow illness by burning an incense called *alucema* in the enclosure of the affected herd. Here again is the idea of odours (with smoke as a medium of transport) that are thought to be effective in driving off the killer spirit. In the same vein, we recall the advice of an old lady concerning sheep plagued with diarrhoea. She recommended making them sleep a couple of nights on some strongly odorous herbage, such as *Hondovalle*, a tropical plant, or *Santa Maria* (Feverfew), a high mountain plant. As stated before, both of these plants are also used in cures and cleansings of other illnesses in both animals and people because of their odorous qualities.

Prevention
Even though difficult to avoid, Michacalan shepherds try hard to keep their herds from being affected by rainbow. They are in fact quite careful to prevent their animals from grazing close to water or near pasture areas that are known to have been touched by a rainbow recently. As two elderly brothers once explained to me: 'One has to take care of the animals so they won't drink bad water, rainbow water. Therefore, one has to tend the animals and keep them always together.'

Another way to protect the sheep from being affected by rainbow consists of building spiritual defences for the animals. This is done by putting horse, donkey or dog skulls on the sides of the corrals where the animals spend the night. Indeed, several corrals in Michacala displayed animal skulls put up on sticks. My *comadre* explained to me how these skulls prevent rainbow from taking animals that sleep under their protection. She said that since these skulls stemmed from strong, powerful, fearless and brave animals during their life-times, their power represented by their skulls were still able to protect the corral animals from rainbow. The skulls also work against other evil forces or spirits.

Bad luck

Another important illness concept in Michacala is called 'bad luck' (Spanish: *mala suerte*), or *chiqui* in Quichua. Sheep that suffer from diarrhoea or that are skinny or sterile may all be afflicted by *chiqui*, as may those that suffer accidental falls. In this, as in all the cases of animal sickness we have reviewed so far, the local diagnosis is quite independent of the symptoms. In general, diagnosis depends on the interpretation of previous events in the life of the afflicted animal. Did it pasture near areas touched by the rainbow lately? Did something extraordinary happen to the owner's family in the last few weeks?

Bad luck is an ailment that is usually caused by the sheep owners, or one of his or her close relatives. Sheep will become sick and die as a consequence of the bad luck of their holders. Michacaleños believe that bad luck befalls a person if he or she leads a bad life, even though, in some rare cases, a person might be born with bad luck.[26] In general, however, bad luck is contracted by a socially offensive way of life; as for example, by committing adultery or being overly aggressive or mean.

A friend once described the main causes of bad luck in a person in the following way: 'If one is unhappy and fights a lot, this is very bad. Such a person becomes ill-fated. Adulterers, those who fight with their neighbours, their spouses, or family – those are very, very *chiqui*.' This informant indicated the following symptoms of an affliction with *chiqui*: 'There are no economic gains, nearly all animals die, money vanishes fast or the children die.' In another instance, an elderly friend explained to us that all his sheep had at some time become barren because he had contracted *chiqui*.

The crucial characteristic of bad luck is that only the property of the afflicted person (or of his family) is truly in danger. That is, bad luck is self-inflicted and self-destructive evil which is not harmful to other people's properties or lives. Among those who suffer most from the bad luck of an afflicted adult are his or her own small children. This is supposedly so because they are the weakest creatures in every household, that is, the ones most prone to the evil influence emanating from a person with *chiqui*. This confirms once again an observation we already made earlier: Michacaleños believe small or young animals (but also small or young children) lack not only physical strength, but more importantly spiritual strength, or *sinchi*. Because of this weakness, they are powerless against evil forces or powers – for example, the bad luck of a relative who lives improperly.

Treatment
If sheep are affected by the *chiqui* of a member of their owner's family, they may get diarrhoea, grow weak, attract parasites, suffer physical injuries through falls, or even get stolen. Treatment of an afflicted animal aims, again, basically at expelling the evil force that has invaded it by contact with the human porter of that force, their owner or one of his or her kin. To achieve that expulsion, villagers apply the very same procedure as in the case of rainbow: they beat the animals with some strong-smelling plants.

Furthermore, we were told of at least two cases in which the desperate owner of an afflicted sheep beat the animal not with plants but with clothing stained with his wife's fresh menstrual blood and even with his own still warm trousers. When we asked why hitting animals with blood stained cloth or warm trousers was supposed to cure animals, afflicted by bad luck, we got the following answer: 'Here we have had experiences and sometimes animals get well. When animals suffer from bad luck it is the same as with humans, it won't go away by itself. Therefore we beat them with trousers.' We thought it was obvious, that this informant was either not willing or else unable to give us a more detailed explanation as to the working of this cure.

We should now ask whether such a treatment makes sense within the Michacalan theory of animal sickness? A valuable hint leading to the solution of this problem comes from the Ecuadorian physician, Dr. Eduardo Estrella, who pointed out that the blood-stained cloth might well symbolize female fecundity to the Michacaleños, while the man's trousers may represent masculinity and overall physical strength. By beating an ailing flock of sheep with these symbols, the female and virile powers might well be thought to be transferred to the animals in question and strengthen their defences.[27]

Prevention
As we have already said, bad luck is an illness-causing power provoked by the lifestyle of the afflicted animals' owner or his kin, but usually of the adult family

head. Prevention therefore requires the pursuit of a socially responsible lifestyle according to local norms. As the most likely human carriers of bad luck, Michacaleños consider these to be those who are quarrelsome, aggressive, unco-operative or adulterous. Such persons will attract bad luck and consequently endanger his or her animals. Following this moral logic, the best preventive strategy in order to avoid animal losses due to bad luck is then simply to comply with the customary rules of proper social behaviour.

Sinister person

A third etiological concept of the Michacaleños we would like to discuss here is *lazipa* (sinister person) because of the insight it will allow us into the Michacalan theory of animal illnesses in general. A sinister person may be called in Spanish someone with *mala espalda* (a bad backbone). *Lazipa* is very similar to the concept of bad luck as discussed earlier, from which it differs only in one crucial respect: people afflicted by *lazipa* don't endanger their own animals, but only those of other people. So while bad luck is self-defeating, *lazipa* is harmful to others.

The way a human being becomes a carrier of the destructive *lazipa*-power is the same as in the case of bad luck: those living a morally unacceptable lifestyle may become afflicted.

Again, a sinister person most often harms small, young, or especially pretty animals. Guinea-pigs are specifically prone to suffer from a sinister person because they are so tiny. Furthermore they live in the kitchens of Michacalan families, where visitors are usually entertained, some of whom may be carriers of the *lazipa*-power. Serious dangers also exist (and for the same reasons) for puppies, which, for example, habitually approach visitors who are potential carriers of this ill-making force. But despite the special susceptibility of guinea-pigs and puppies, any other animal species and even small children can be affected too.

A villager once told us about his friend's small, pretty foal which had been killed by the *lazipa* of an afflicted neighbour. The neighbour had been in a nearby village where he had argued with some people and returned home still furious. On his way home, he passed by the animal, transferred his evil power to the foal which then became sick. The despairing owner of the animal tried to cure it by hitting it with his trousers and several plants, but the foal died anyway.

Not everybody who has had a fight or who has become angry for some reason necessarily turns into a sinister person. One of my *compadres* illustrated this fact for me by describing a day he had a fierce fight with his wife. He left the house enraged and passed by a young, pretty goat. Immediately, he said to himself: 'Let's see whether the little animal will die?' Fortunately, nothing happened to the animal. This experience did not, of course, seriously shake the firm belief of my compadre in the existence and harmfulness of *lazipa* as, after having told others of the incident, he immediately went on to relate the recent death of some of his guinea-pigs to the visit of an infuriated neighbour a few days before. He concluded that not everybody's anger is necessarily dangerous to animals, but only the anger of certain people – namely those who not only are momentarily enraged but who suffer more enduringly from bad temper as a personality trait.

Treatment

In the case of guinea-pigs afflicted by a sinister person, the female owner will most probably collect stinging nettles and scatter them on the kitchen floor so that the sick animals have to run over them. The idea behind this curious method of treatment is that the nettles irritate the malign *lazipa* spirit so much that it finally leaves the animals it has invaded. But in young animals such as lambs, foals and calves, stinging nettles alone are not enough. Instead villagers apply the same treatments as for the rainbow and bad luck afflictions; that is, they drive off the illness-causing spirit by beating the animals with powerful plants or other materials.

Prevention
Knowledge of the etiology of sinister person dictates the measures to be taken to prevent the affliction. Herders attempt to protect their animals from this sickness by keeping them away from any people who are potential carriers of the evil power. In so far as any belligerent neighbour or visitor might constitute a health threat to one's flocks, people avoid living in crowded residential areas. Indeed Michacaleños prefer to live in somewhat isolated compounds. Living too close to a frequently used trail is also avoided, as the frequency with which people pass close by one's animals increases the likelihood of their being struck by *lazipa*. To prove the correctness of these ideas, one villager told me that her sheep were much better off since she moved her household from a more densely settled sector of the village to the isolated and distant one.

As *lazipa* specifically attacks pretty animals, some owners of such animals try to make them look uglier by rubbing them with ashes from their fireplaces. Another preventive method is to put collars around the necks of beautiful young animals. We were told that these colourful collars function somehow as traps for the looks of an angry bypasser, deflecting them from the animal itself. Obviously, Michacaleños believe that *lazipa* is especially easily transferred to its victims by eyecontact.

Witchcraft

A last local illness etiology that we will present here is witchcraft, referred to in Quichua as *pucuna* (Spanish: *soplo*). The Michacaleños suspect witchcraft to be the cause particularly of rare or highly virulent diseases. Some years back, for example, the free-ranging cattle in Michacala suddenly got sick and died one after another. According to the villagers, the animals showed some sort of hoof-rot and had pouches on their tongues which prevented them from eating. The Michacaleños did not know what particular illness had befallen their cattle (most probably foot-and-mouth disease), and so they suspected witchcraft. As animals of numerous villagers became affected, the outbreak of this disease was indeed considered a witchcraft attack by a non-villager against the entire community.

In the case of any sudden loss of animals (by whatever cause in the veterinary diagnostic system), witchcraft is a possible local diagnosis. A village friend once told me about how witchcraft is carried out. He pointed out that the person who wants to harm the flock of his enemy, collects some of the droppings or samples of wool of the target herd, which he then brings to a sorcerer. The sorcerer will blow over the items with cinnamon, cigarette smoke and eau-de-Cologne, putting a spell on the whole flock in this way. The target herd will develop diarrhoea or other nasty symptoms. In any case, death will follow fast.

Treatment
Whenever witchcraft is diagnosed, the Michacaleños do not attempt to cure their animals themselves. In these cases, help can only come from a specialist, that is,

from another sorcerer, or healer. The healer's method of saving the animals from the killing spell is to send the spell right back to where it came from. Thus, it is essential to identify the sender of the magic spell. When we asked our informants how the village reacted to the above-mentioned case of witchcraft against their community, the answer was that they hired a sorcerer (Spanish: *brujo*) to find out where the evil magic had been sent from and to send the spell straight back.

All villagers affirm that now, without the help of a sorcerer, there can be no salvation for a bewitched flock. But at least one old lady told us that her father had known how to cure an evil spell without consulting any sorcerer at all. She told us that he used to prepare a broth of fox meat, fish, guinea-pig and some herbs from the tropical coast and the Amazon lowlands; among them, what she called *Jaya Huasca* (we guessed that she was referring to Ayahuasca, *Baniopsteris caapi*). She considered *Jaya Huasca* an excellent remedy against an evil spell, and she added, giggling: 'If humans [cristianos] drink it they get drunk, and it is good against witchcraft.' Once cooked, the broth prepared by her father with the ingredients mentioned above had to be force-fed to the sick animals, and was said to be infallibly effective.

Prevention

Witchcraft directed against the animals of a villager is meant to kill. Someone affected by witchcraft must therefore try to identify someone who might be sufficiently malevolent to trouble himself to do such serious harm as instigating witchcraft. Sources of enmity, serious enough to cause an enemy to hire a sorcerer, include fights over land, deliberate crop damage or theft, marital jealousy, inheritance quarrels and fraud. Logically this means that to prevent witchcraft one has to prevent making enemies who are willing to engage and pay for black magic as a method of revenge.

Can this specific constellation of ideas coming under the heading of witchcraft in Michacala also be integrated into the local health model that we started to outline on the basis of such concepts as rainbow, bad luck and sinister person? We think so.

Principles of the indigenous model

All the illness etiologies we have discussed up to this point, human and veterinary alike, contain valuable information about the Michacalan picture of the make-up of the world in general. According to this image, certain places such as rocks, waterfalls and creeks, or plants[28] and even the moon or rainbow, hold powers or spirits that can either threaten the health of animals (and even humans) or help them to recover from illness.

Another important principle of the Michacalan theory is that any animal (or person) normally has enough power of its own to ward off the external evil influences that constantly threaten all living creatures. In fact, animal health according to this ideology[29] is very much the result of a continuous and necessary balance between external spiritual powers and the animal's inner spiritual force in Michacala. A strong animal is able to keep evil powers at bay even if it comes into close contact with them, while a weak animal will be penetrated or taken (Quichua: *japishca*) by it, even if contact is only casual or at a distance. An animal already weak not only gets taken more easily, but also rapidly becomes further weakened by the alien force until its spiritual agony is manifested in the symptoms of its illness and eventually its death.

Interestingly, the inner spiritual power of animals in general is considered fairly weak – though still sufficient for survival. It is definitely much weaker, for example, than in adult humans. As we stated earlier, in their relative weakness animals resemble children, and like them, are considered incapable of surviving without close surveillance by responsible humans.

The amount of spiritual strength attributed to specific animal species in Michacalan thought depends on a few basic conditions. First, Michacaleños judge the inner strength of an animal species and also that of an individual animal on the basis of its physical strength, expressed generally in height, aggressiveness and body-weight. The taller, more aggressive and heavier an animal is, the stronger it is considered spiritually. Accordingly, horses, cattle and mules are considered much stronger than llamas, which in turn are believed to be more powerful than pigs or sheep. As we saw above, that extra strength might sometimes be harnessed to protect other animals weak by nature.

Another basic condition determining an animal's relative strength is age, as new-born and young animals are always considered much weaker than adults. In fact, young animals are believed to have hardly any spiritual defences at all, which is why they die so easily. With age, of course, they can acquire more physical strength and, in the case of children, also more wisdom and judgement and thus will be able to defend themselves better against external illness-causing agents.

A third criterion for determining inner spiritual strength is aggressiveness or ferocity. Wild bulls, wild horses, very stubborn mules or especially aggressive dogs in Michacala are considered to possess more power than quieter animals of the same species. These animals can actually fend for themselves, which is why it seems safe to the Michacalan people to let their horses and cattle, for example, roam freely in the high *paramo* areas.

Knowing all this, we can appreciate better why Michacaleños consider with some resignation sheep to be one of the most vulnerable animal species in the village and why they expect their mortality rate to be much higher than other animals.

Sheep are surpassed in weakness only by guinea-pigs, which are considered even more vulnerable to illness-causing spiritual forces. So weak are guinea-pigs that they are not allowed to leave the kitchens of their owners where they are at least relatively protected from threatening external spiritual forces. Although, again, the Michacaleños habitual living space, the family kitchen, exposes the guinea-pigs to illness-causing powers carried by visitors. Thus, guinea-pigs are the most frequent victims of bad luck and sinister person. In a certain sense, they can even be said to absorb the evil power carried by such people before it attacks children or other somehow weakened members of the family. It is in this sense that guinea-pigs are believed, in fact, to possess a health-securing function in Michacalan families.

The receptivity of guinea-pigs to malign powers is shown in another important use of them within the Michacalan health system. As throughout the Andes, guinea-pigs in Michacala are also customarily used in ritual cleansings and the diagnosis of human illness. For diagnostic purposes, a guinea-pig is rubbed over the body of an ailing person until it dies. Then the guinea-pig is cut open and its internal organs are carefully investigated by the healer to identify deformations and other clues considered significant for the specific ailment of the patient. Underlying this use of guinea-pigs, of course, is again the idea that spiritual forces can be transferred from one thing or person to another by contact, generally in the direction of the stronger to the weaker. In this case, the evil forces that are at work in the sick patient can be transferred into the guinea-pig by the rubbing, thus supposedly producing a visible malfunction in its internal organs that can then be interpreted by the knowledgeable healer.

In curing an animal of an evil force that has invaded it, the basic idea is to drive the evil force out of the animal's body – for example with strong odours. In this case, it is the strength of the odours in question that are most important. To the Michacaleños, the strength of the odours represents the amount of spiritual power inherent in a smelly substance; a power that can be used to ward off and even chase away any evil opponent. Not just substances that prove their strength by their strong smell, but in fact all substances considered somehow powerful in themselves can be used to counter malign powers or spirits.

In fact, at the heart of the Michacalan medical and veterinary theory there seems to be an equilibrium theory of powers that can be either positive or negative to the patient. All carriers of positive powers can be used as curatives, while all carriers of negative powers are potentially health-threatening.

At this point, we should mention a concept we have dealt with in Chapter 1 and which is central to the field of human and animal health in Michacala. In the anthropological literature, this concept is known as the hot–cold syndrome. We will discuss it here only in passing because it illustrates the principle of balanced powers that we find so essential for understanding the deep structure of Michacalan views on health in both animals and humans.

According to the Michacalan version of this theory, the health of an animal, or a person, depends on maintaining a certain temperate state of their bodies. Some external agents cause – in symbolic terms – a thermal imbalance in humans or animals making them thus unwell. Moonlight and rainbow, for example, are not only considered (somewhat humanized) spiritual forces that may take animals but they are also considered cold agents; that is, if they penetrate a body, they may also cause a thermal imbalance in their victim, cooling it down. Flatulence, for example, is also often interpreted by the Michacalan villagers as a symptom of thermal imbalance towards the cold side caused by moon or rainbow. In serious cases, excessive inner coldness is said to result in inside rot (Quichua: *huicsa ismuchi*) which can lead to death.

To be effective against thermal imbalance in a sick animal or human being, cures, of course, have to counterbalance the excessive cold or heat that has penetrated the patient. When there is too much cold, for example, only remedies that are considered 'hot' or 'warm' can be used. Alcohol, lemon juice and pepper sauce are such 'warm' or 'hot' items that may cure an excess of coldness caused, for example, by being invaded by the rainbow. Thus, lemon juice and cane alcohol are sometimes force-fed to sheep when they have diarrhoea accompanied by flatulence. Here we recall the woman friend, mentioned in Chapter 1, who cured flatulence in her sheep by putting pepper sauce into the anus of the poor animals, a choice of remedy that reflects the same cultural logic – but does not make any sense from a veterinarian's point of view.

The same is true for some of the other curative actions we observed in Michacala that would dismay a vet. Some herders, for example, put lard on the navel of neonate lambs. According to the villagers, this has to be done if there is a shining moon. The logic behind the use of lard is that lard is supposed to ward off a cold agent, like moonlight, from getting into the body of the neonate through its weakest spot, its navel, which, like a wound, is an opening through which any illness-causing force can enter easily. Lard is also put on castration wounds in rams for precisely the same reason.

In Michacala, then, the hot–cold syndrome, on the one hand, and ideas about illness-causing spirit agents (like rainbow, sinister person and bad luck) on the other, are all variants on the more general idea of health as a balance of inner and outer forces. An imbalance of these forces of whatever kind produces certain symptoms in the afflicted animals and people, though there is still argument in Michacala as to what type of symptoms can be attributed to what type of external agent. This gives any diagnosis of animal and human illness in this village considerable flexibility.

We find it especially noteworthy in all this that Michacaleños seem to have no difficulty at all in fusing into one thought system two etiological theories which, on first sight, seem so fundamentally different from each other as the hot–cold syndrome on the one hand, versus the theory of spirit agents on the other.

Both theories are used in this village as simply two different ways of talking about balance and imbalance of external and internal spiritual powers in animals (as well as in humans); that is: they both refer to one and the same epistemological framework. It so happens that most spiritually strong plants and other remedies possess at the same time always some thermal qualities in the Michacalan world-view, too. Therefore, they can be applied consistently to most illnesses diagnosed in the village according to either model. Still, it is important to remember that Michacaleños view hot–cold imbalances and illnesses caused by the different spirit agents as distinctive types.

To recap what we know about Michacalan health model and curative theory: the most varied remedies can be used in the treatment of illnesses, as long as they counterbalance the negative spiritual power that is afflicting an animal or human. For example, garlic, coriander, disinfectants, llama urine, and kerosene are all smelly substances that can be used to make harmful spiritual powers uncomfortable and make them leave the animals they plague. Even beating a sick animal, or bedding it on nettles, is sometimes considered an effective route to this result. In both cases, power (of the man beating an animal, or of the nettle) is transferred onto the animal imbalanced by some negative spiritual agent. This implies, of course, that the evil spiritual powers afflicting animals are somewhat personalized in Michacalan thought, as they are thought to be equipped with certain quite human likes and dislikes, and even a sense of pain, so that they can be bullied into certain desired behaviour.

This is also why villagers consider rubbing an animal suffering from keds with kerosene or some disinfectant to be effective. What the Michacaleños hope to do by this procedure is to drive off the most probable cause of that infestation: the rainbow spirit.

Testing the model: protective witchcraft

A sensible test case for the Michacalan theory just outlined, which typifies the view that health is a result of the balance of inner and outer forces in animals and people, is protective witchcraft.

In Michacala, protective witchcraft is an important measure for spiritually strengthening and thereby protecting one's flock, so that it does not attract any evil spiritual agent. Protective witchcraft is intended to prevent an evil affliction of an animal by the transfer of positive power. This is done by a professional sorcerer, called a *yachac* (literally: he who knows). When a *yachac* puts a protective spell on the flock, this is supposed to increase its spiritual defences against evil influences. In other words, it is hoped that the spell may prevent the animals from becoming spiritually imbalanced (that is ill) and that it will therefore allow the flock to multiply.[30] Such protective sorcery is paid for by the animal's owner.

Numerous villagers freely admitted to believing in the efficacy of such witchcraft and gave as proof the names of fellow villagers who possessed more sheep, llamas or other animals than others and who were thus suspected of having paid for protective witchcraft. Villagers, however, did not admit to practising this type of witchcraft for their own flocks, as witchcraft in general is considered unacceptable here.

How protective witchcraft is done was once described to us by a villager whose relations had followed the procedure. He explained: 'One has to get a bowl first. Then you go and get some sheep wool and put it into the bowl, then you add grains of quinua, barley and beans. Then you go to the sorcerer and you ask him, "please, be so kind to blow on this so my animals won't die and will increase." Then one pays 12 or 15 thousand sucres and the herd will increase. Later, at home, you bury the bowl in the corral ground.'

How is this concept of protective witchcraft (or of witchcraft in general) integrated into the Michacalan theory of health as a balanced state of interior and exterior forces in living beings?

As Michacaleños see it, sorcerers are able to perform both black and white magic. In fact, it is this double potential of any sorcerer which makes it morally dubious for Michacaleños to even admit consulting any sorcerer, even for protecting their own flocks, as such consultations will arouse suspicion in fellow villagers as to their true intentions. This is of course so because black and white magic are, technically speaking, fairly inseparable procedures. During either sort of witchcraft, spells are attached to an item that belongs to the intended victims and will have to be returned to them later. The crucial role of witchcraft, then, seems to be that the sorcerer somehow adds a spiritual power to an object which has none inherently. This power, by way of contact or closeness, will then influence the balanced state (or health) of the target. It may influence it either positively, by adding spiritual strength, or negatively, by taking strength from it. As we indicated before, the underlying logic is that a spiritually weakened being is more likely to develop an illness.

Sorcery, in Michacalan thought, consists then of a double feat: first, it means attaching spiritual powers to an object; second, and much more important, it means selecting either positive or negative powers that will then be attached to that object. But this, of course, is the very secret of all medical lore in Michacala. A woman who attempts to cure an excess of coldness in an animal by forcefeeding hot foods, or who tries to counteract the debilitating influence of rainbow over her flock by beating it with a man's trousers, is in fact doing the same thing as a sorcerer: she is trying to counterbalance a negative (cold) force by adding a positive (or hot) one.

At the heart of all these actions, then, is a theory, or world-view, shared by Michacaleños, which postulates the existence of powers that are sometimes attached to certain objects, sites, or even humans themselves. These powers may influence the inborn force of any other living being either positively (strengthening it) or negatively (detracting from it) and thereby making the creature ill. Only a few objects possess positive forces by nature. Remember, for example, the skulls of strong animals to be found in numerous sheep corrals in Michacala. Here, the physical strength of an animal (which, as we already saw, is a positive force in Michacalan thought), is represented in its very skull. Its force protects the sheep that spend the night in the corral by adding its strength to that of the sheep, helping them to resist invasive evil powers.

Sinister people and bad luck, on the other hand, work on the basis of the same logic as does black magic. In the case of *lazipa* and *chiqui*, negative powers emanate from some human beings. So, the concepts of *lazipa* and *chiqui* teach us how good or evil powers are conceptualized in Michacalan thought. Sinister person and bad luck are clearly self-provoked illnesses, that is, brought on by the afflicted human beings themselves. Of what, then, does the affliction consist? It seems that the persons afflicted with these illnesses transfer their (negative) strength (mostly by contact and physical closeness) to their final victims, unbalancing their inner state of being. As mentioned before, such negative power is acquired by an immoral lifestyle, which is believed to unbalance the interior strength of a person in a very peculiar way: it augments one's negative interior forces to the extent that they themselves may finally become unbalancing even to a third person or an animal.

In a certain sense, then, people can gain individual power simply by behaving improperly, though such power is negatively loaded and in turn can badly affect others. Indeed, in Michacaleño eyes, acting selfishly and egotistically or ignoring social and communal demands on one's time and resources leads to the accumulation of negative powers; such negative strength is dangerous to the health of other people and animals.[31]

Our argument then is that Michacalan conceptions of white and black magic, of hot–cold illness, and of external spiritual agents, all belong to the same general model of health as a consequence of a balance of internal and external powers. We are dealing here with a central element of the Michacalan worldview which can be rendered in various guises and versions.

Obviously, to Michacalan eyes, everyone possesses both good and bad powers – just as a sorcerer does. These powers are in fact part of their make-up. They are in local parlance their life-power, strength or *sinchi* – in itself composed of positive and negative components. In a normal, healthy individual these components are believed to be in a state of balance but they may easily become unbalanced, either by external agents or by a change in lifestyle. What sets ordinary people apart from sorcerers is that ordinary people cannot control the positive or negative components of their life-force at will, nor attach them to other objects. In other words, they cannot manipulate the life-force of other people according to personal intent as a sorcerer can.

Still, one can accumulate positive and negative powers by leading a certain lifestyle. A morally irreproachable lifestyle increases positive inner powers. Thus a morally upright individual will develop his or her interior strength to the fullest, so much so, that a well-known weakening spiritual agent like rainbow, mountain or wind will not unbalance him or her nor easily afflict their children or animals. But ordinary people's powers can also be negatively unbalanced by an improper lifestyle. Such people become negatively strong and therefore eventually dangerous to others.[32]

This model of balancing hot and cold, internal and external powers, as basic determinants of health and illness in Michacala, may also be applied to other fields outside the arena of animal health management. For example, this model works not just in the veterinary field, but also in the arena of human medicine. It can also be tested further by application to our analysis in Chapter 2 of the relationship between Michacaleños and their environment.[33] The illness concepts presented here, such as evil wind, taken-by-the-mountain and *tingu* have to be understood from the angle of an underlying theory of clashing forces. In fact, the theory of balancing powers stands at the very heart of the Michacalan world-view.

Conclusion

Numerous IKS researchers have lately pointed out that many agricultural practices observable in non-western societies are in fact effective, if judged from a purely technical point of view, although these practices may be explained by the indigenous people in mystical-magical terms.[34] Though we strongly sympathize with the main thrust of this argument, it cannot be denied that one has to concentrate on the local customs that can be found to be somehow effective according to formal-scientific standards. Therefore, we may read about medical herbs used by this or that ethnic group that have been found to be effective in a western medical sense; or, we read about often adapted cropping practices that are shown to counter certain environmental deficiencies of this or that locale.

We hasten to add that we do not doubt the value of these observations, but we seldom hear of means and practices that turn out to be ineffective or counterproductive if analysed from a scientific point of view, as such observations would only strengthen the prevalent negative assessment and prejudice about the capacities of non-western cultures – an outcome anthropologists have good reasons not to further. However, as it seems then, local knowledge and practices that cannot easily be shown to be effective are either ignored or brushed aside in those studies as residuals of false knowledge in otherwise highly efficient thought systems.

Consider this issue by again taking up the example of the rainbow illness in Michacalan sheep. Rainbow, as you may recall, is believed to contaminate pasture areas in Michacala where it has touched the ground, detectable in the form of multi-coloured puddles, river waters or swampy areas. Science maintains that the marshy pampas of Michacala are in fact ideal breeding grounds for parasites. Animals which graze in these areas are therefore very likely to become infested either by ingestion or through wounds. As a result, more animals are likely to suffer from symptoms like diarrhoea, flatulence and infection. What might be assumed is that the Michacalan herders effectively avoid those marshy areas, although they are not aware of the micro-biological dangers lurking there.

Such seems to be the argument made by McCorkle (1989), who, in her valuable study on sheep production among agro-pastoralists in highland Peru, has pointed out that the peasants she investigated correctly linked the excessive humidity in certain pasture areas to certain endo-parasitic illnesses. She takes this as proof of the accuracy of farmers' observational skills. As we see it, this may well be so, but then she would certainly have difficulties in explaining why Michacalan herders, for example, lead sick animals into a gorge and beat them there with certain herbage whenever they are allegedly taken-by-the-rainbow. Nor would it be easy to explain what sense it makes to put hot pepper sauce in the anus of a parasite-infested sheep.

Maybe one can find an acceptable scientific explanation for some of these strange treatments. But we doubt very much that anyone can find explanations, which satisfy scientific criteria, for all of them. Yet the ethno-theory we have elaborated above as an instance of the Michacalan world-view does, in fact, explain the described treatments consistently in native terms, and seems therefore a better way to understand local veterinary practices.

We will present one final and telling example of the importance of expertise on local knowledge and theory for understanding animal management practices in a locale like Michacala. One of my project colleagues who worked with me closely for over a year in Michacala was a specialist in guinea-pig production. Besides his many other tasks, he also tried to convince Michacalan people to change the way they used to breed guinea-pigs. Generally, guinea-pigs of both sexes and all ages in this village share the earthen kitchen floor. My colleague tried hard to convince the villagers to change this and to separate their animals according to sex and age. Furthermore, he wanted the animals taken out of the kitchens and put in shelters of their own for hygienic reasons. On the basis of such improved management he expected the peasants to be able to genetically select for the biggest and healthiest animals which he believed would certainly improve the meat production for family nutrition.[35]

After weeks of searching in vain, my colleague finally found a volunteer for his programme who, incidentally, was the village president at that time. This was considered an extremely good omen by my colleague, as local leaders often function as brokers of innovations in their communities. He quickly installed the man's guinea-pigs in a separate hut of the president family's compound.

Weeks later, I was in conversation with the village president. We were talking about the concept of sinister person, which I had trouble understanding. The president tried to explain to me how it is that animals might suffer from sinister person. He mentioned that his own guinea-pigs had until recently suffered a lot from this sickness, especially since he had become president of the community. As such he was frequently visited by villagers complaining to him about an estranged husband, angry relative or envious neighbour. Angry, aggressive villagers can easily acquire the sick-making sinister person syndrome, which they may then bring to someone else's cooking hut during a visit. The village president actually believed that this had killed most of his once numerous guinea-pigs. He then pointed out to me that he had now solved this problem with the help of my colleague, by finally evacuating the guinea-pigs from his kitchen where those visitors usually arrive.

The fact that my colleague had actually been able to convince this man to change the management of his guinea-pigs towards a scientifically rational mode could be, and was in fact, seen by my colleague as proof that development counselling actually works, even without proper knowledge of a people's theory. But to look at the example in this way creates a false picture of what actually happened. As we saw, the village president did not change his way of keeping guinea-pigs because he somehow recognized the superior expertise of my colleague in these matters, or the breeding and hygienic advantages of what he was told to do. He did so because the suggestions of this zoo-technician made sense to him in terms of his own evaluation of his situation, in which the dangers of *chiqui* and *lazipa* are important factors influencing the president's decision-making.

Now, we may ask if it is really necessary to know a people's theory of animal health in such depth in order to guarantee an adequate understanding of local animal management and to suggest acceptable changes to the peasants? Why should it not be enough to analyse indigenous practices only within a scientific framework, and sort technically good from bad practice, and then somehow teach locals to change the bad ones? Isn't the ideological system of the Michacaleños, after all, just their way of explaining to themselves what they simply cannot understand better?

Due to our research results and experiences we argue that development agents that do not take local knowledge, culture, and theory seriously will never be able to control the change processes their interventions are going to produce among the development clients.[36] We hasten to add that we do, of course, not argue in favour of more cultural expertise in order to control the results of the developmental encounter, or to make developmental action work. We only argue that knowledge of local culture is a precondition for improved communication and co-operation between socially and culturally distinct peoples who hold different truth claims about the world around them and the way it functions.

Fortunately enough, the philosophy of developmental action has lately accepted the principle of dialogue and participation as indispensable in any developmental encounter (cf. Pottier, 1993: 11–12). But true dialogue and participation cannot be implemented and function by the willpower alone of all participants in the encounter. High-quality knowledge about the cognitive differences between both parties as well as communication methods are necessary for constructive dialogue and democratic participation. Which other changes in our attitudes and communicative abilities are needed to get an action-generating dialogue started will be the subject of the following chapter.

6 Hungry for Hope: on the cultural and communicative dimensions of development

IN THE PREVIOUS TWO chapters, we described the knowledge of agricultural experts, on the one hand, and of indigenous peasants on the other as two distinct cognitive systems and ethno-theories. This documentation serves to explain the relative unresponsiveness of Michacalan peasants (and by extension, of many other indigenous groups) to many development suggestions. We argue that such unresponsiveness can frequently be attributed to the fact that much of the advice and assistance offered to indigenous people does not make sense if judged from the perspective of their own theory and experience.

This position gives rise to two questions: one, how can we decide whether developers' or indigenous knowledge is the more appropriate to solve the agricultural problems in a specific locality? And two, is it reasonable to pose the first question like that? In what follows, we will reflect upon this issue in two steps.

First, we will present three positions toward evaluating culturally distinct modes of thought, such as so-called primitive and scientific theories, by reviewing the rationality debate of the 1950s and 1960s. Evans-Pritchard, Robin Horton and Peter Winch elaborated different theoretical positions about the validity of primitive modes of thought that can still be found in contemporary discussions of indigenous knowledge systems. This is why we consider the rationality debate still relevant to contemporary social theory.

In the second step, we advance a novel understanding of rational action, namely as bound to the mode of communication. This proposal is grounded in arguments provided by Paulo Freire and Jürgen Habermas. We conclude by relating their suggestions to methodological advances made by indigenous knowledge systems research and participatory approaches to development.

The rationality debate

The issue of any sort of value-laden comparison between culturally distinct modes of thought reminds us of a famous debate about the rationality of different modes of thought. This debate among social scientists and philosophers took place during the 1950s and 1960s and is well documented in Wilson's *Rationality* (1970), and in Horton and Finnegan's *Modes of Thought* (1973). Their discussion highlights endeavours to find criteria for defining the degree of rationality of any mode of thought.

The cornerstone of the rationality debate had been Evans-Pritchard's rightly famous discussion of *Witchcraft, Oracles and Magic among the Azande* (1937), which in itself constituted a clear advance on previous works on primitive thought by Edward B. Tylor, James George Frazer, Emile Durkheim, Bronislaw Malinowski and Lucien Lévy-Bruhl. In these latter's works, magical thinking, for example, had generally been interpreted as a pre-logical mode of thought (especially in Frazer and Lévy-Bruhl) or as a kind of inferior science (in Tylor). Alternatively, it was considered a primitive religion or, last, as a functional response to some psycho-social need.[1]

Dismissing implicitly all of these judgmental interpretations, Evans-Pritchard evaluated Azande ideas by emphasizing instead the overall logical coherence of their magical thinking, comparing it favourably with the logical coherence of scientific thought. Fully aware of the epistemological difficulties that arise when members of distinct cultural communities meet, Evans-Pritchard argued that mutual acceptance and understanding is the only possible way of truly communicating with each other.

With this, Evans-Pritchard had put his finger on the weak spot in intercultural communication: namely, the need to overcome the epistemological differences in order to establish a good dialogue. He explains why mutual acceptance is fundamental to high-quality communication: 'You cannot have a remunerative, even intelligent, conversation with people about something they take as self-evident if you give them the impression that you regard their belief as an illusion or a delusion' (1976: 244).

Obviously, Evans-Pritchard already recognized that an ethno-centric attitude towards the knowledge of another people constitutes, in fact, the foremost obstacle to effective intercultural communication. However, even if we accept another people's cognitive system as logically coherent and conforming to their subjective experiences of reality, open questions remain:

o How can interaction between people of different cultures holding contradictory views on reality (that are both well justified by the totality and inner logic of their respective thought systems) take place?
o Can their interaction ever be based on something other than the imposition of the views of one party on the other?
o Is such imposition ethically justifiable?

These questions were discussed by the participants of the rationality debate with special reference to Evans-Pritchard's pioneering work. One of these participants was Robin Horton, who contributed the notable essay, 'African Traditional Thought and Western Science' (1970).[2] He remains close to Evans-Pritchard's position, emphasizing first the formal-logical resemblance between primitive and scientific modes of thought; and second, insisting that all kinds of thought systems represent valid alternatives to tackle the complexities of reality. In fact, Horton highlights the functional equivalence of supernatural and scientific thought systems: 'Like atoms, molecules, and waves, . . . the gods serve to introduce unity into diversity, simplicity into complexity, order into disorder, regularity into anomaly' (1970: 134).

Horton insists not only that the similarity of science and religion is limited to their logical and explanatory qualities, but that there are further similarities on empirical grounds. He asks:

Are . . . traditional notions of cause merely artifacts of the prevailing theoretical idiom, fantasies with no basis in reality? Or are they responses to features of people's experience which in some sense are 'really there'? My own feeling is that, although these notions are ones to which people are pre-disposed by the prevailing theoretical idiom, they also register certain important features of the objective situation. (1970: 137)

This is in fact a significant variation on Evans-Pritchard's position in so far as for Horton, primitive thought is not only logically consistent, but reflects the empirical experiences of indigenous people made in the course of their lives. To make his case more plausible, Horton uses the example of malaria, to which Africans seem to have acquired a limited resistance, transforming it into a deadly threat only in times of extreme stress:

In these circumstances the traditional healer's efforts to cope with the situation by ferreting out and attempting to remedy stress-producing disturbances in the patient's social field is probably very relevant. Such efforts may seem to have a ludicrously marginal importance to a hospital doctor wielding a nivaquine bottle and treating a non-resistant European malaria patient. But they may be crucial where there is no nivaquine bottle and a considerable natural resistance to malaria.   (1970: 138)

In other words, Horton argues in favour of the effectiveness of some traditional knowledge. In the end, he considers religious modes of thought to be logical, coherent, sometimes empirically correct, as well as capable of giving meaning to people's everyday experiences. However Horton still considers science superior to all other cognitive alternatives, whenever a choice has to be made between scientific and religious modes of thought. The problem then remains: what shall we do if some local knowledge and practice is not re-interpretable as being effective from a scientific point of view? Are we then right to impose our scientific truth on other people even though their ideas or practices are fully justified and logical within their own world-view?

A negative answer to this question has been put forward from another participant in the rationality-debate, namely Peter Winch (1970). In his essay *Understanding a Primitive Society*, Winch rejects any attempt to evaluate magical thought from the perspective of scientific standards of observation, quantification and validation. Instead he argues that to compare aspects of a magical knowledge with aspects of a scientific knowledge is to commit a category mistake (Winch, 1970: 93). By borrowing from Evans-Pritchard's ethnographic material, Winch explains why such category mistakes are committed so frequently in cross-cultural contexts, even by well-trained researchers. He writes:

. . . the African Azande hold beliefs that we cannot possibly share and engage in practices which it is peculiarly difficult for us to comprehend. . . . An anthropologist studying such a people wishes to make those beliefs and practices intelligible to himself and his readers. This means presenting an account of them that will somehow satisfy the criteria of rationality demanded by the culture to which he and his readers belong: a culture whose conception of rationality is deeply affected by the achievements and methods of the sciences, and one which treats such things as a belief in magic or the practice of consulting oracles as almost a paradigm of the irrational.   (1970: 78)

A category mistake, as understood by Winch, consists in trying to explain another culture's beliefs in terms of one's own beliefs. The author instead compares scientific and magical modes of thought to language games borrowing the concept from Ludwig Wittgenstein in order to illustrate his opinion that it is meaningless to compare two different games. In other words, just as it is foolish to compare the rules of chess with the rules of backgammon, it leads nowhere to evaluate a magical language system from the perspective of a scientific one.

Winch's writings represent a relativist position against scientific positivism and argue for the co-existence of multiple realities. This author proposes that magical and scientific thought systems are not just distinct, but also incomparable. For him, magic or science constitute alternative epistemological frameworks that can be evaluated only on the basis of their own criteria of effectiveness and proof. According to Winch, any attempt to do otherwise, that is, to compare particular aspects of distinct cognitive systems, is in itself an irrational endeavour. He explains this accordingly: 'Something can appear rational to someone only in terms of *his* understanding of what is and is not rational. If *our* concept of rationality is a different one from his, then it makes no sense to say that anything either does or does not appear rational to *him* in *our* sense' (1970: 97).

Winch's approach to looking at distinct modes of thought as contrasting language games has influenced our presentation of formal-scientific and indigenous knowledge of agricultural production in the *paramo* community of Michacala in the previous two chapters. The purpose was to illustrate the systemic character as well as the dissimilarity of scientific and indigenous views, that remain surprisingly unnoticed or underplayed in the minds of many development practitioners. Or, to paraphrase Winch, we have tried to show that indigenous farmers and agricultural professionals indeed play different language games.

Does this mean that we have to give up all hope for constructive communication, participation and sound social interaction in inter-cultural encounters? Winch, seems to imply just this. According to him, people can only act within their own language game and, whenever the language games of two or more people turn out to be incommensurable, attempts to prove one (or aspects of one) superior to the other are futile; any such attempt will never convince all the players involved. Therefore, participants in cross-cultural encounters seem condemned to fight out their differences, or leave each other alone.

From Winch's point of view, democratic communication and action in intercultural encounters are logically impossible as any contact between players of different language games can only end in competition and dispute in determining whose game should be played. Ineluctably, players who finally impose their rules on the other side can never ascribe their triumph to any inherent logical superiority of their ideas or practices, but only to the superior amount of power they were able to command at the moment of the encounter. In this view then, cross-cultural encounters always inevitably boil down to power games in which one of the parties involved finally has to suffer the frustration of seeing things imposed on them against their will. We feel that this particular implication of Winch's argument leaves us without hope to confront and master the challenges posited in the modern world in which multi-cultural interaction has become – and will remain – a constant feature.

To us, instead, the fundamental problem of intercultural co-operation is rooted in the fact that interactors with different cultural backgrounds tend to declare another people's cognitive system as inferior to their own. By doing so, they actively destroy any constructive interaction with the members of a distinct culture, other than by force. The only way to escape the vicious cycle is to accept another people's world-view as being as valid as one's own, and – on the basis of that acceptance – to enter into a kind of dialogue from which power is excluded as the decisive catalyst. Intercultural communication and interaction without recourse to power still has to be tried and we believe with others that this can be the most exciting social utopia toward the end of the second millennium.

Dialogue and change

Paulo Freire's thinking about a revolutionary pedagogy of cultural emancipation is continuously rediscovered by western intellectuals (McLaren and Leonard, 1993). Freire's book *The Pedagogy of the Oppressed* (1984) lays the foundation for a challenging theory of education for the poor and illiterate in Third World countries. Freire argues with respect to literacy programmes that it is possible to attain cultural synthesis between the teachers and their illiterate students. To reach this goal, it is first necessary to admit the differences between their world-views, instead of ignoring, repressing or substituting them.

Only by becoming aware of the distinct world-views of teachers and their students, can they begin to generate dialogue about how to co-operate in a self-conscious and reflective way (Freire, 1984: 183). Clearly, contrary to Peter Winch's message about the incompatibility of different language games, Freire represents a philosophy of hope which maintains that revolutionary change can be planned and accomplished by uneducated people and is possible even in non-revolutionary societies (Aronowitz, 1993: 17–19).

When Freire formulates his thesis, he has his native Brazil of the 1950s in mind, with its unjust socio-economic and political structures. He points to the particular role and responsibility of teachers in preserving an unjust *status quo* by obstructing the development of self-awareness, confidence and respect in their students, especially if these are illiterate adults. Education, Freire complains, has degenerated into a system of knowledge transfer from educators to students at the expense of true dialogue.

Freire passionately criticizes the teachers' conviction that only they have any valid knowledge about the make-up of the world, arrogantly disregarding their students' knowledge and thus, obstructing a personally and politically liberating learning experience.[3] He even argues that the teachers' displayed superiority constitutes a violent act against students' intellectual and cultural integrity, and denounces it as an aggressive form of cultural invasion by the latter. Explicating the essence of this concept of cultural invasion, he writes:

> In this phenomenon, the invaders penetrate the cultural context of another group, in disrespect of the latter's potentialities; they impose their own view of the world upon those they invade and inhibit the creativity of the invaded by curbing their expression. Whether urbane or harsh, cultural invasion is thus always an act of violence against the persons of the invaded culture, who lose their originality or face the threat of losing it (1984: 150).

What Freire criticizes so passionately in Third World education reminds us in fact of many development and extension programmes. During most extension programmes, socially and culturally different people meet, and the developers are trying to convince their clients of new and different ways of thinking, acting and producing without ever taking their clients' views into serious consideration. According to Freire, the unawareness of the others' world-view is all that is required to violate the other group's self-esteem. And we may add in his own words: 'Such a program constitutes cultural invasion, good intentions notwith-standing' (1984: 84).

What makes Freire's thesis even more interesting is his proposal for forging non-invasive encounters. Dialogue, he states, is the condition for making learn-ing an empowering personal experience. The ultimate goal of such dialogue, however, is to achieve a cultural synthesis between those involved in the encoun-ter, and we may add, for example, between development professionals and indigenous peasants: 'In cultural synthesis, the actors who come from 'another world' to the world of the people do so not as invaders. They do not come to *teach* or to *transmit* or to *give* anything, but rather to learn with the people, about the people's world' (Freire, 1984: 181).

For Freire, dialogue has virtually therapeutic qualities and decidedly eman-cipatory and political functions within a socially and culturally divided society like Brazil. Dialogue is the main means to raise an oppressed people's self-awareness and self-esteem, eventually allowing them to identify and solve their own problems in a constructive and self-empowering manner. The political and social power that Freire assigns to dialogue, make his reflections especially akin to the work of the German philosopher Jürgen Habermas (Figueroa, 1989: 110–13). Habermas, like Freire, considers communication to be the only legitimate means for determining social interaction and making rational choices in the face of growing social conflicts in today's world.

Communicative rationality

Since the 1970s, Habermas has elaborated a paradigm for rational communication and action.[4] According to Habermas, the need for this new paradigm is based on the deficiencies of prior attempts during which rationality became too narrowly understood to represent instrumental or strategic rationality, at least within the occidental philosophy (1984a: 143–243). Habermas and many others argue that this distinctively modern equation of rationality with instrumental-strategic behaviour and thought has ultimately failed to explain social development adequately. Because of this, a variety of extreme anti-rationalist viewpoints have become the frustrated answers to the failed 'occidental project' which depicted human social development as heading towards the victory of rationality (Hollis and Lukes, 1982). Giddens (1987: 55–6) exemplified the drastic shift from predominantly positivist orientations in the social sciences to decidedly relativist perspectives by referring to Winch's publication *The Idea of a Social Science* (1958). Winch's messages were seen as essentially untenable in the 1960s, while they have become acceptable in the 1980s. As an alternative to thriving relativism, Habermas calls for a fundamental paradigm shift in social theory from strategic to communicative rationality. In other words, Habermas asks us to direct attention to rationalizing the conditions for uncoerced communication and consensus across distinct views for safeguarding rational interaction. He labels this kind of rationality as 'communicative rationality':

> This concept of communicative rationality carries with it connotations based ultimately on the central experience of the unconstrained, unifying, consensus-bringing force of argumentative speech, in which different participants overcome their merely subjective views and, owing to the mutuality of rationally motivated conviction, assure themselves of both the unity of the objective world and the intersubjectivity of their lifeworld.   (Habermas, 1984a: 10)

In his endeavour to redefine the meaning of rationality, Habermas goes back in time to when the majority of sociologists and philosophers were still interested in rational behaviour or speech. He reproaches them for defining reason in narrowly strategic and purposive terms. Habermas traces such a limited understanding of rationality back to Max Weber who suggested the separation of rationality in its instrumental, normative and aesthetic elements. Tracing this tripartite concept from Weber to the present, Habermas complains that even the representatives of the Frankfurt School unfortunately swallowed the Weberian hook by conventionalizing the view that rationality is basically equivalent to instrumental reasoning and action, putting normative and aesthetic criteria aside. Habermas concludes that it is the equation of rationality with instrumental action that has finally led to an increasingly pessimistic turn against everything that is good in the enlightenment project.

As an alternative to this pessimism, Habermas demands a new orientation in social theory away from its mistaken focus on instrumental rationality to communicative rationality and henceforth from instrumental action to communicative action. Communicative action, as defined by Habermas, is action which is oriented toward reaching an agreement (i.e. illocutionary act) and, as such, is clearly distinguished from action that is success-oriented (i.e. perlocutionary acts).[5] 'I count as communicative action those linguistically mediated interactions in which all participants pursue illocutionary aims, and *only* illocutionary aims, with their mediating acts of communication' (Habermas, 1984: 295).

In this novel view, a mode of thought or behaviour can be labelled rational as far as it facilitates a democratically achieved consensus through uncoerced communication. Accordingly, for Habermas, the rationality of any society, and the relative level of progress reached in its historical development is measurable not in terms of its technical, economic or civilizing achievements, but mainly by the ability of its members to solve social conflicts discursively, that is, by generating consensus through the use of communication channels.[6] To be able to open such communication channels, or keep them from clogging up, Habermas considers it indispensable that societies develop institutional and structural conditions that allow their members to discuss and exchange ideas and arguments in truly uncoerced ways. It is in this respect that he sees modern society and its specialized planning institutions as especially deficient and even dangerous to democracy.

For Habermas, decision-making in modern societies has become increasingly relegated to a professional class of bureaucrats and technocrats who take vital decisions for society as a whole but are independent from the people. Not surprisingly, for Habermas, recent German history, before and after World War II, is the principal example of this negative social development (Horster, 1990: 124). Standing in the dialectical tradition of the Critical Theory as reflected in the works of Theodor Adorno, Max Horkheimer and Herbert Marcuse, Habermas also views bureaucracies and corporations with profound suspicion, highlighting their tendency to develop into social subsystems[7] that claim increasing autonomy, justifying that claim with a supposed need for functional efficiency. Having inherited the preoccupation with the decay of democratic fundamentals from the Frankfurt School, Habermas denounces the growing independence of bureaucratic, industrial and techno-scientific social subsystems from normative-moral considerations as a threat to democracy. In *Technik und Wissenschaft als 'Ideologie'* (1981), he deals explicitly with the issue of how engineering, science and democracy can be intermediated and linked back to the consensus of acting and critically debating citizens.

In this endeavour, Habermas' communicative action approach corresponds to Freire's dialogical approach, in so far as both point to the generative, or therapeutic potential of communication. But there are also important differences between the two thinkers. One of these differences is that Freire demands a change in the character dispositions of educators towards their students, or of political leaders towards their followers. To him, the ideal dispositions that allow for dialogue are: love, humility and courage in interaction with people (1984a: 124). Some critics have accused Freire of putting too high a demand on the character disposition of those involved in education, calling the way he defines the conditions for true dialogue as idealistic (Figueroa, 1989: 92).

It is precisely in this respect that Habermas surpasses Freire because the former defines the conditions for communication less in terms of the personal dispositions of the speakers involved, than in terms of the formal structure of the

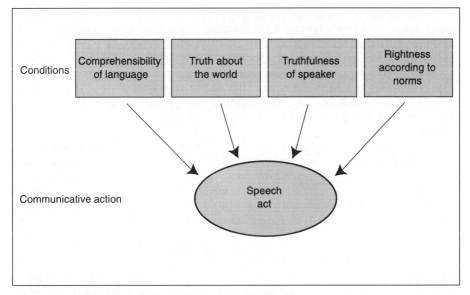

Figure 3   *Four conditions for communicative action*

communicative situation. He does so specifically in his two-volume work on *The Theory of Communicative Action* (1984a) in which he outlines a 'universal-pragmatic infrastructure of speech and action'.[8] For Habermas (1976: 215), the infrastructure of speech acts (meaning, 'I do things in saying something') is made up of four conditions, or validity claims, as he prefers to call them, following John Austin. These four validity claims have to be fulfilled in every speech act in order to produce an agreement between speakers which, in turn, is the only legitimate basis for human interaction and co-operation (Habermas, 1979).

The first of these validity claims is that speakers must use linguistic expressions that are intelligible and comprehensible to their listeners. This precondition is called the validity claim of comprehensibility, and asks that two speakers use a language and language expression known by both if they want or need to com-municate effectively with each other. The second validity claim is that speakers must say things about the world as they know it.[9] Habermas calls this condition the validity claim of truth. The third condition for communication is that speakers must sincerely mean what they say, so listeners are able to trust them. This is the validity claim of sincerity, or truthfulness. The fourth and final condi-tion for communication is that speakers must choose language and behavioural expressions that do not offend their counterparts; that is, that they are nor-matively, morally, and tactfully acceptable to the listeners. This is the validity claim of rightness (Habermas, 1979; 1983).

Habermas knows, of course, that most everyday communication lies in the grey areas in between these claims as most speakers do not consciously reflect on all four validity claims to make sure that they are involved in true commu-nication (1979: 3). In fact, the four validity claims define only the ideal conditions of communication, or speech acts, that have to be met in order to lead to rational consensus and interaction. However, he suggests that such ideal conditions can be met – a proposal that is regarded with much scepticism by many social scientists.

The advantage of this model is that the validity claims as defined by Habermas help systematically to examine and structure public and private dialogue.[10] In the case of dissent and conflict, both clear signs of a failure to generate consensus, the model provides criteria for analysing why the communication process has been interrupted. It allows us to analyse the failure of communicative action better by distinguishing whether the root of the communication problem lies at the level of comprehensibility, propositional truth claims, personal sincerity, or the moral correctness of what has been expressed, by whom and to whom (Habermas, 1983: 148).

The ethnographic chapters document the great potential for miscommunication at the level of propositional truth claims in multi-cultural contexts, in which, for example, agricultural specialists and Andean peasants try to interact. We recognize that experts as well as peasants assess truth claims by considering what is said with what they know (or believe to know) about the make-up of reality. Such cross-checking is not an easy endeavour in inter-cultural encounters because messages are exchanged that are true only relative to the specific world-view held by that speaker. Yet recognizing this fact does not automatically prohibit the possibility of communication. The Habermas model suggests that one condition indispensable for communication and co-operation – even across a cultural divide – is an a priori acceptance that what others claim in verbal or non-verbal expressions does indeed constitute truth for them and has to be treated as sincere.

We therefore argue that the failure to communicate in development projects often does not refer to any intended omission by development agents in talking and listening to their clients – although such omissions may be at the root of it as has been argued elsewhere (Salmen, 1987). Instead, we emphasize another kind of communication failure developers are often guilty of, namely, that of being unable to achieve mutual understanding and agreement with their clients on what the latter hold to be true.

A major obstacle to improved inter-cultural interaction is that many development agents still believe their main task consists in transferring – supposedly superior – scientific knowledge and technology to their clients who supposedly lack adequate knowledge. This transfer model of knowledge leads to basic mistakes that occur from the very beginning of their encounter with indigenous people. Confronted with statements and practices of their clients that make no sense to agricultural professionals, they assume that these statements and actions do not represent knowledge, but instead reflect its absence. Or, alternatively, developers considered rural people's opinions – if expressed at all – to be false beliefs or superstitions. But by considering a people's knowledge as devoid of truth, the developers violate exactly what Habermas identifies as one condition for rational and legitimate co-operation.

An important step towards constructive dialogue and co-operation in any development encounter is to accept a people's ideas and practices as their operating knowledge and way of experiencing and interpreting the world. This presupposes the developers' acquaintance with local theories and practices; in other words, developers need to acquire a certain amount of cultural competence. A complementary step on the part of the developers must then be to treat their own scientific knowledge about reality as just another interpretation of reality on a par with that of their clients. This means that the experts have to refrain from the ever-present temptation to treat scientific knowledge as *de facto* superior to their clients' one. Instead they have to enter the encounter willing to treat the indigenous views on reality as equally valid as their own, even if according to local opinion anti-parasitic injections cool down sheep, eventually making them sicker and killing them (Chapter 1). This done, the developers may be able to enter an uncoerced exchange of ideas with their clients, to identify and define alternatives to conventional actions and fields of co-operation that are meaningful to both parties. A sensible alternative could be to treat sheep orally against internal parasites.

Getting hungry for hope

Development science has made much progress recently in fields related to indigenous knowledge systems research and participatory appraisal and planning methods. Such progress has become possible due to the failure of mainstream attempts to foster development by transferring knowledge and know-how to the clients of projects. The demonstrated inadequacy of a transfer model has made most development disciplines increasingly interested in local knowledge and technologies. This turn of interest is healthy and has found expression in a growing number of publications and networks concerning indigenous knowledge and participatory methods (Brokensha et al., 1980; Richards, 1985; Warren et al., 1995; Theis and Grady, 1991; Cernea, 1991; Pretty et al., 1995). The success of IKS and PRA approaches is impressive and finds expression in a rapidly spreading demand for culture-sensitive training of developers.

Slowly, participatory approaches find their way into the academic communities and curricula. Chambers attributes this phenomenon to the fact that 'PRA parallels and resonates with paradigm shifts in the social and natural sciences' (Chambers, 1994b: 1437). He sees a certain commonality between participatory approaches and perspectives in postmodern social theories because 'all affirm and celebrate multiple realities and local diversity' (1994b: 1449). We agree but wish to add that PRA methods contribute uniquely to bridge distinct worldviews, and thus give a practical response to the postmodern postulate of co-existing realities. That participatory methods bring people with different cultural backgrounds closer together has caused great excitement among development practitioners and indigenous people alike who have experienced their action-generating impact.

The development of participatory methods, however, accompanies the embryonic emergence of a social paradigm which we described above as communicative action, or consensus theory. We find that some participatory tools like *GRAAP – Groupe de Recherche et d'Appui pour l'Autopromotion Paysanne* (i.e. a group to research into and promote self-help among peasants in Bobo-Dioulaso, Burkina Faso) or Road to Progress conform to certain demands of that consensus theory. Participatory methods help to structure the communication process between people in a democratic way. They help powerless people to speak up and evaluate their situation self-critically, no matter what their level of formal education. PRA methods, for example, facilitate reaching an intersubjective consensus which generates the stimulus to co-operative action among those participating in the discussion. Developers are facilitators in the communication process which requires a thorough acquaintance with the culture and experience of the participants. Recognizing the complementarity between communicative action theory, participatory methods, cultural and communicative expertise, we suggest that these approaches, jointly, can pave the way to an innovative understanding of intercultural communication and co-operation on a large scale.[11]

The main asset of such a joint venture is that it responds to an urge for hope that intercultural co-operation can be accomplished democratically and peacefully. This challenge is growing to the extent that an increasing number of people belonging to distinct cultures interact due to the facilities provided by modern communication technology and to the rules of an expanding international economy. In the process, we encounter a dazzling array of opinions, values and truth claims.

Today, many people need hope that such diversity can be constructively dealt with in an open and democratic fashion. This book is intended not to give a final answer to this quest, but to bring hope to those who find inter-cultural communication and development a most exciting field. A field to face a basic challenge at the end of the millennium: namely, to identify social theories and methods which help to promote mutual understanding and legitimate co-operation between culturally and socially distinct peoples. Considering the concepts and ideas, presented above, we believe that it is, indeed, a good time to get hungry for hope.

Notes

Chapter 1

1 The *Proyecto de Fomento Ganadero* (PROFOGAN) was financed by the Ecuadorian Ministry of Agriculture (MAG) and the German Agency for Technical Co-operation (GTZ) between 1985 and 1992. It aimed at improving production, management and marketing of animal products. A first step towards this goal involved the detailed study of existing animal production systems of small-farmers in six different ecological zones of Ecuador, ranging from the tropical coast to the high Andes and into the Amazon region of this country. The *paramo* of Zumbahua became the sixth and final research zone to be studied by the project.

2 With 270 000 sheep, the Province of Cotopaxi was the second most important sheep producer in Ecuador in 1987 (PROFOGAN, 1988: 52).

3 The hot-cold concept is popular in Latin America. For a general review of the illness concept see: Anderson, 1987; for Mesoamerica, see: Foster and Gallantin, 1978; López Austin, 1984 and Vogt, 1976; for the Andes, see Hahold, 1988; Estrella 1977, Bastian and Donahue, 1981 and Bastian, 1989.

4 Good (1994) argues that whose people's insights are considered beliefs and whose are considered knowledge is an expression of the power differential between those people without and those with knowledge.

5 'Outsiders are people concerned with rural development who are themselves neither rural nor poor' (Chambers, 1983: 2).

Chapter 2

1 See Asad (1973) and Pathy (1987) for harsh critiques of anthropology's involvement in the colonial episode. For a more balanced, yet still critical account, we recommend James (1973).

2 See Maybury-Lewis (1988), Robertson (1984), Swantz (1985), Bennett (1988), Haswell (1975), Grillo and Rew (1985).

3 Recently, Dyson-Hudson denounced a still prevalent view of pastoral people in Africa as behaving irrationally: 'Formerly they were thought to be the one nonrational group of participants. Although this view is fading, there is still a tendency to regard pastoralists' lack of response as due to perversity rather than to flaws in the project design or unreasonable demands to take risks for unknown and undemonstrated benefits' (1991:249).

4 See for example: Chambers (1983; 1991); UNDP (1993); Pottier (1993).

5 *Road to Progress* has been developed by two colleagues from the Institute for Rural Extension and Communication at the University of Hohenheim, Willi Ehret and Andrew Kidd. They used features of various participatory methods such as a visualizing appraisal method called *GRAAP*. This method is named after the NGO in Burkina Faso that developed it: *Groupe de recherche et d'appui pour l'autopromotion paysanne*. Other elements for *Road to Progress* were taken from an approach known as *LePSA* (*Learner-centred, Problem-posing, Self-discovery, Action-oriented*) which was developed by *MAP International* (*Medical Associate Professionals*).

Chapter 3

1 *Paramo* is the name of the high Andean ecology (Monasterio 1980), characteristically consisting of low-growing shrubs and yellow-greenish grasslands
   which are used as natural pasture for extensive animal husbandry. In Ecuador, these grasslands can be found approximately between 3200 and 4700
   metres above sealevel (Acosta-Solís, 1984; Cañadas, 1983).

2 We use the denomination white, black and indigenous in Barth's (1969) sense
   of ethnic categories auto-ascribed by the local people themselves. Today,
   most of the peasants of the parish classify themselves as indigenous (Spanish:
   indígena; Quichua: *runa*).

3 The total number of communities in the parish is controversial. Some, for,
   example count La Cocha as one huge community, while others consider it
   made up of several smaller ones. Such lack of definition has to do with the
   hacienda past of the parish as a whole during which these settlements did not
   represent historically grown indigenous populations, but represented hamlets
   that fulfilled specific labour tasks for the hacienda. In comparison, the community of Michacala which we have studied has a well-defined territory as it
   once was a small hacienda of its own, bordering with the hacienda of Zumbahua. The count of 10 communities follows suggestions made by the peasant
   organization, UNOCIZ, which we consider a legitimate representation of the
   parishioners' viewpoint.

4 *Cholo* in Ecuador identifies an indigenous person who has advanced economically and socially by having a job that secures a regular income. This is
   mostly achieved by way of trading activities and by living in a parish or
   canton town, and by speaking Spanish. The typical *cholo* distances himself
   ideologically from his indigenous roots (compare Fuenzalida-Vollmar 1971).

5 For an excellent analysis and interpretation of local food symbolism and its
   ethnic and political connotations, see Weismantel (1988).

6 The price of a hat ranged from 5000 to 10 000 sucres while a well-fed sheep
   cost around 8000 sucres (US$14) in 1989.

7 These market scenes recall Scott's (1985) discussion of powerless peasants,
   who have no other way of resisting exploitation by landlords or merchants
   except by 'foot-dragging' and obstinate endurance.

8 Sugar-cane liquor is one of the best selling products during the market day.
   A bottle of *tragu* is even cheaper than one of Coca-Cola, which makes it
   easily shared between kin, friends, merchants and customers during the
   market day.

9 For illuminating new ways to discuss hacienda history in Ecuador, see Guerrero (1991) and Ramón (1990; 1987). Guerrero analyses in a dialectical and
   hermeneutic way the interactions between the dependent indigenous labour
   force and the hacienda, based on ethno-historical hacienda records and ethnographic research. Ramón (1990) elaborates on ethnohistorical information, and constructs a first draft of an 'Andean Project' that might serve as a
   model for a new multi-ethnic constitution of Ecuador.

10 See Oberem (1967) and Guerrero (1991) for a closer review of the position of
   huasipungueros and *yanaperos* in Ecuadorian haciendas.

11 According to indigenous informants, they received *huasipungos* from only one
   to seven hectares. According to a study from the 1960s by Costales and Costales, they held two to 29 hectares per family (cf. Weismantel, 1988: 66). Based
   on today's stratification of landholding, all these different indications could

have been correct but for different sectors of the hacienda. Still today, certain communities have a much higher average holding per family than others.

12 Winterhalder, Larsen and Thomas (1974) were the first to discuss the crucial importance of dung as fertilizer and fuel in high-altitude communities. In my study community, animal dung is exclusively used as manure. One hectare of land used for potato production will be fertilized with some 180 quintales (8300 kg) of dung (Hess, 1992: 76)

13 A different system to control distinct and distant ecological zones is known in Andean literature – after Murra (1972) – as 'archipelago' land use. This kind of long-distance land use can still be found today in southern Ecuador among the Saraguro Indians (Belote and Belote, 1985).

14 Based on our census data, we calculated that out of infants died within the first year of life.

15 *Compadres* is the relationship between the natural parents of a child and his or her godparents.

16 The customary proportion of a harvest to be given to helpers is, for example, a short hundredweight (Spanish: *quintal*) of barley as a return for three days of harvesting. A day's help in excavating shallots should be compensated by half a sack of the produce, while a day of labour in the bean harvest should be compensated by at least three large bunches of the plant. Finally, two days of help with the potato harvest should be repaid by roughly one short hundredweight to the helper.

17 Compare Gudeman's well-known essay on *compadrazgo* in which he explores godparenthood as a relationship that has economic as well as spiritual and symbolic connotations (1971).

18 This slogan of solidarity has often been used in indigenous protest marches in Ecuador during recent years.

19 This is a rule, frequent in other societies also; for example among the Tzotzil-Maya in Chiapas (personal communication by Professor Evon Z. Vogt, Jr.).

20 Tubers such as potato, *melloco*, *mashua* and *oca* are the most frost-resistant crops in a cold mountain environment. In Michacala, we find a total of 12 varieties of potatoes. These are: *Leona, Tacanguilla, Yana Leona, Corondilla, Murungu, Semichola, Norteña, Silo, Pargati, Uchu rumi, Uvilla* and *Muru punchu*. However, there are few varieties when compared with reports from villages in the southern Andes of Peru, where the average farmer grows up to 35 varieties (Brush et al., 1981, cf. Franquemont, 1990).

21 'Wild' cattle are untamed and range freely in distant *paramo* areas. They are borrowed for the popular bullfights that take place during certain festivals in Michacala, Zumbahua or neighbouring parishes.

22 McCorkle (1983) described in detail such an animal boarding system in Peru; for Ecuador we have found a brief sketch of a similar system close to Guamote (Gangotena 1981).

23 Guillet (1980:16) has aptly argued that the prevailing understanding of production and exchange in the Andes as adaptive has become tautological in much anthropological writing about the Andes.

24 See Palmer (1992) for a comprehensive collection of essays about the Shining Path movement.

25 See classic contributions to the topic of Andean adaptation: Murra (1972), Alberti and Mayer (1974), Masuda, Shimada, and Morris (1985) and Golte (1980).

26 Ecuadorian Confederation of Indigenous Peoples; or in Spanish, Confederación de Nacionalidades Indígenas del Ecuador.

27 Worsley (1984: 193–4) criticized the image of the poor, hopeless, impotent, apathetic or dependent peasant. Worsley argues that the debate about a supposed 'culture of poverty', inspired by the work of Oscar Lewis (1959) on Mexican lifehistories, is only an expression of ethnocentric middle-class views about poor people in general.

Chapter 4

1 With the help of a villager, we took daily minimum and maximum temperature readings from October 1989 to October 1991 at 3800 m. The thermometer was fixed 1.9 m above ground level, protected from the sun. Precipitation was also recorded daily. The lowest monthly average temperature during this period was 6.7°C in August 1990 and the highest 8.5°C in June 1991.

2 In Michacala, the lowest night temperature measured during two years was –3°C and the warmest 6°C. In turn, the lowest day temperature has been no higher than 7°C and the highest 18°C. The permanently low temperatures in the village are subjectively perceived especially harsh during windy, cloudy and humid days, even though the objective temperature measurements prove that dry days are objectively lower.

3 The average annual temperature in Michacala is 7.7°C, and annual precipitation is 665 mm.

4 Twenty-five per cent of all infant deaths during the last three decades were attributed by families to the evil wind.

5 McKee (1988: 232) studied infant illnesses in the Ecuadorian highland province of Bolivar and mentions that people imagined that supernatural evil travels through the air and is attracted by fragrant smells, as well as repulsed by bad-smelling odours. Interestingly enough, in the eastern United States children once used to wear bags of foul-smelling *asifetida* for the same purpose as noted in Mark Twain's *Tom Sawyer* (Personal communication, Jane Hilowitz).

6 In Spanish, this illness is popularly called *cogida de cerro*.

7 In other parts of Ecuador, the concept of being taken-by-the-mountain has sexual connotations. This is because the verb 'take' (Spanish: *coger*; Quichua: *japina*) can be used to refer to sexual intercourse or rape (Estrella, 1982). But Michacaleños do not perceive of a woman taken-by-the-mountain as having had intercourse, willingly or not, with a mountain spirit.

8 According to Pérez, who did an extensive study of toponymies in the Province of Cotopaxi, "Quitsahua' is a Colorado term and means, 'to make really big'; in Spanish this is *'hacer bien grande'* (1962: 103–7).

9 Michacaleños consider pregnancy an illness (Quichua: *uncui*). It puts women in a state of greater emotional stress. In other contexts, emotional distresses such as mourning and grief are also considered dangerous to human health, weakening the mourner. Also, Tousignant (1988) has elaborated upon the fact that the indigenous people of Bolivar Province consider sorrow to be a serious cause of illness. From Peru it is reported that sorrow may inflict a loss of one's soul (Crandon-Malamud, 1991: 28).

10 Strathern (1981) once argued for the Mt Hagen people in Papua New Guinea that females are ideologically linked to the private domain and devalued in the public one because men effectively control the public domain and larger social activities. This statement also seems to be true in Michacala.

11 Reiter (1975) observed a similar attitude among southern French housewives.

12 In Andean ethnography, *tinkuy* is the name for ritual dance-battles during which antagonists meet in violent union (Allen, 1988). Allen also pointed out that the word has wider applications: 'When streams converge in foaming eddies to produce a single, larger stream they are said to *tinkuy*, and their convergence is called *tinku. Tinkus* are powerful, dangerous places full of liberated and uncontrollable forces' (1988: 205–7).

13 See, for example, van den Berg (1990).

14 For example, *lancha* is a plague that attacks tubers, or more specifically the leaves of tuber plants. It is a fungus (*Phithoptera infestans*), whose appearance is encouraged by excessive humidity.

15 Two-thirds of all answers to the question 'When do frosts occur?' indicated months that pertained to the rainy season.

16 Nash (1993: 123) in her work on indigenous tin miners in Bolivia also explained the miners' offerings to the *Tío* ('Uncle' or the spiritual owner of the mines) as their way to gain his goodwill, so they could extract the ore from the mine without being punished, i.e. killed, in the process.

17 For a thorough discussion of the syncretic-symbolic appropriation of the Christian cross by the Maya-tzotzil and Maya-tzetal de los Altos de Chiapas, see Vogt (1990).

18 Other case studies in Ecuador, like the one by Campaña (1991) used to discuss religious festivals in terms of social and economic interests of their sponsors (Spanish: *priostes*). Botero (1991) emphasizes the significance of the indigenous religious festivals in Ecuador as ethnic markers of resistance to the dominant religious culture and ideology of *mestizos*.

Chapter 5

1 For a discussion of sustainability as an important development concept, see Redclift (1987); for a discussion of sustainable development strategies in the Ecuadorian Andes, see Bebbington (1993).

2 Corkill and Cubitt (1988) cite average annual rates of inflation of 6 per cent (1965–73), 18 per cent (1973–84), and 35 per cent (1987). According to our own experience, the upward trend continued to 50 per cent (1989–1991).

3 The demographic pressure in *paramo* areas is not the only reason for the disappearance of the natural vegetation cover. The conversion of grasslands into cultivated areas is often directly promoted by agricultural programmes. The idea of agriculture as the most important means of making an Andean landscape productive is deeply rooted in the mentality of development planners in ministries and in NGOs.

4 Compare Gilles and Jamtgaard (1982).

5 Andean animal species such as *alpacas* and *vicuñas* are not bred in Ecuador, with the exception of a few experimental farms belonging to the Ministry of Agriculture and some private *haciendas*. Llamas which are used as beasts of burden can still be found in a few scattered pockets of the highlands, but mostly in impoverished indigenous parishes with an inadequately serviced transport system.

6 See Lipton (1977), Johnston and Kilby (1982: 39–40).

7 Using a proposal by Johnson (1978), we imagine a system as a conceptual construct. A system is made up of components which are interrelated and which constitute a closed model. Which elements are considered important depends, however, on the specific approach favoured by a researcher.

 8 Flores Ochoa (1968, 1977b, 1979, 1988), Browman (1974), Inamura (1981), Orlove (1977, 1981a, 1981b), Flannery, Marcus and Reynolds (1989), Thomas (1977), Webster (1973).

 9 For veterinary information, we used the handbook on sheep science by Ensminger (1970). Naturally, we owe many valuable insights to our colleagues in PROFOGAN.

10 Michacalan sheep are generally plagued by numerous diseases, low fertility (only 61 per cent of mature female sheep reproduce in a given year), high mortality (every sixth adult sheep dies each year; half of all lambs die during their first year).

11 Two zoo-technicians used the linear transect method. From the data derived by this method, the botanical composition of the entire communal *paramo* has been calculated in terms of number of species and in terms of their surface coverage. See Hess (1992: 79).

12 Basically, these are Compositae such as *Lucilia aretioides, Baccharis servillifolia*; Rosaceae such as *Alchemilla orbiculata*; and Polygonaceae such as *Eriogonum pyrolactolium*.

13 For a detailed listing and a more accurate presentation of the surface coverage of each these plants, see Hess (1992: 79, Table 12).

14 This idea resembles the concept of fright (Spanish: *susto*) as a cause of illness in humans. In much of Ecuador, fright is said to lead to soul loss and may ultimately cause the death of the afflicted. Fright and subsequent soul loss are widespread illness concepts throughout most of Latin America (Rubel, O'Nell and Collado, 1985) and, in fact, in many other parts of the world too (Good and Good, 1982).

15 One of the first to shift research attention to this aspect of livestock production was Winterhalder, Larsen, and Thomas, 1974. The archaeologist Wing (1986) even argued that it was the urgent need for fertilizer in high Andean agriculture that most likely stimulated the domestication of llamas and alpacas around 2500 BC.

16 PROFOGAN's vet, Dr J. Herrera, gave his opinion on all products used in the local treatment of sheep ailments.

17 The latter is a widespread popular anti-diuretic infusion, usually used for people who suffer from diarrhoea.

18 The literature on hot–cold theory in the Americas is indeed vast, and it usually concerns only issues of human health (Foster, 1976; Hahold, 1988; Logan, 1977; Messer, 1981; Boster and Weller, 1990).

19 Personal communication by Carlos Olivo, *mayordomo* of the hacienda of Zumbahua during the last 20 years of its existence.

20 See Parsons (1945), Estrella (1977), Aguiló (1987), Balladelli (1990).

21 Muñoz-Bernand (1986: 143) describes the case of Pindilig, in the Ecuadorian Province of Cañar, where locals consider dangerous only the reflection of the rainbow in the water, not the water itself.

22 For example, flatulence in an animal signals that it is 'putrefying inside'. Such flatulence is attributed to the intrusion of some cold agent such as moonshine, a cold wind, or the rainbow. Such intrusion is facilitated when the animal is wounded, either by accident or after castration. That is why the avoidance of moonshine phases for castrations is such an important issue.

23 The rainbow can affect all other animals species too, which then receive the same treatment as the one described for the sheep. Especially endangered are smaller, younger or wounded animals.

24 The English translation is taken from White (1982). Unfortunately, we could not find translations for *Tetera* and *Hondovalle*.

25 In the case of sterility or lowered fertility of an ewe caused by rainbow, the above treatment is not recommended. An informant stated that one can cure the rainbow-stricken ewes of their sterility by massaging their bellies with crushed coriander and garlic. In this case, it is the strong odour of these plants which is thought to drive the rainbow spirit out of the afflicted animal.

26 This is a mirror image of what West (1988: 199) reports about Bolivian Aymara and their reasoning about having luck.

27 A method to cure a person who has attracted bad luck and hence has become a danger to his or her family economy and happiness is to take a shower in an ice-cold waterfall in the Zumbahua area, which, according to an informant, has the power to 'wash off' the bad luck. There, one must bath as many times as necessary until one's luck changes.

28 For example, Sola (1992) reports from a neighbouring parish of Zumbahua, Sigchos, that people attribute to tough, spiny, and pleated plants the thermic quality of 'heat', which means that they can be used to cure a 'cold' illness.

29 'Ideology' here stands for a symbolic system that structures awareness of the world and supplies people with orientations for their behaviour (Kahn, 1985).

30 In Michacala, there are no family or communal rituals to help to increase herds, as they are reported for the central and southern Andes. There, numerous ethnographers reported on ceremonies to give offerings to the mountains, which are considered the original owners of the llamas or alpacas which populate the *puna* (Flores Ochoa, 1988; Flores Ochoa, 1977a; Tomoeda, 1988). In the case of Michacala, similar origin myths of herding animals are unknown.

31 Conversely, it is also possible to accumulate positive inner strength by pursuing a good life-style which heightens one's defences against evil attacks of all sorts. For an interesting study of Andean indigenous cosmology and equilibrium theory, see Classen (1993).

32 The idea that moral and social inadequacy can trigger mental and bodily afflictions is indeed widespread throughout many cultures (Kleinman, 1980; Hunt, 1992; Galt, 1991; Herzfeld, 1981).

33 Maybury-Lewis (1989: 15) proposes the existence of a dualist mode of thought structuring all pre-modern thinking. This mode of thought emphasizes the importance of keeping things in a state of equilibrium, while a scientific mode of thought emphasizes process and change.

34 See studies on vegetation (Brokensha and Riley, 1980), crops like rice (Richards, 1985) or potatoes (Brush, Carney and Huamán, 1981). On herding, see McCorkle (1983).

35 Guinea-pigs in Michacala and most indigenous highland areas are one of the most important sources of meat in a household. As meat in general is very rare, it is reasonable to assume that villagers have a vested interest in healthier and bigger guinea-pigs.

36 Ferguson (1990) pointed out that development projects in Lesotho regularly failed to attain their goals. However, development projects none the less had side-effects (many unintended by the projects) that benefited some social groups.

Chapter 6

1 For careful treatment of the differences between these theorists concerning the issues of science, magic and religion, see Tambiah (1990).

2 For an assessment of this classic essay which anticipated criticisms 15 years following its publication, see Horton himself (1982). In our opinion, his review of the original essay is not substantial but rhetorical, refuting most criticisms levelled against it as ungrounded.

3 For a critique of Freire's prediction concerning the liberating potential of praxis by dialogue, see Walker (1981).

4 Habermas elaborates the paradigm of communicative rationality within a model of societal evolution. We share a critical distance from the evolutionary stage model with other contemporaries, yet without necessarily denying the remaining value of Habermas efforts to construct a grand theory (cf. Braaten, 1991: 3).

5 The distinction between illocutionary (geared toward understanding) and perlocutionary acts (geared toward success) is taken from Austin's work on 'speech acts' (Habermas, 1984a: 279).

6 Compare Figueroa (1989: 112).

7 'Subsystems' embody the purposive-rational action of occidental rationality such as the institutions of the modern state and industry (Habermas, 1984a: 144).

8 The most succinct elaboration of the conditions to communicative action can be found in the essay 'What is universal pragmatics?' (Habermas, 1979: 1–68).

9 We admit that we take Habermas in this thesis further than he himself would permit. Habermas would not accept mythical or magical thoughts to be rational truth claims on which a rational consensus should be reached (Habermas, 1981: 79f; 1984b: 470). We clearly disagree with this author and criticize, with others, his position as ethnocentric and scientistic (McCarthy, 1991: 136f).

10 We cannot agree with Ferrara (1990) who argued that Habermas' model of discourse analysis is applicable only to public, but not private discourse.

11 For an interesting collection of essays on participatory communication, see Servaes et al. (1996)

Glossary

adobe	loamy brick
alma	soul
aya	soul of a dead person
cabecera cantonal	county seat
cabildo	communal council and term to address council members
canton	county
chocho	lupine
cholo	a person of indigenous origin who advanced economically and socially by engaging in commercial activities.
comadre	female god-parent
compadre	male god-parent
compadres	god-parents; term of address and ritual relationship between parents and god-parents
comuna	see *comunidad*
comunidad	village, legally recognized by the Ministry of Agriculture
conjunctivitis	eye infection of humans and animals, producing temporary blindness
cordillera	mountain chain of the Andes
– cuna	plural suffix in Quichua
enteritis	infectious disease in sheep caused by excess humidity in the enclosure where the animals pass the night
faena	specified labour task
finca	small farm
gringo	North American or European
hacienda	a large agricultural and livestock estate
hectare	10 000 square metre or 2.47 acres
huasipungo	a plot of land given to a labourer of a hacienda to produce crops for his family's subsistence
huasipunguero	individual who received the use-right to a plot of land, i.e. *huasipungo*
mashua	Andean tuber (*Tropaeolum tuberosum*)
melloco	Andean tuber (*Ullucus tuberosum*)
mestizo	a person of mixed American and European descent
minga	communal, collective labour party
oca	Andean tuber (*Oxalis tuberosa*)
paramo	humid high mountain grassland, found in the northern Andes; in Ecuador it is located between 3200 and 4700 metres
parroquia	parish
puna	dry mountain grassland, found in the central and southern Andes
quichua	language of the Incas; diverse dialects of Quichua are spoken throughout the Andean countries
quinoa	protein-rich Andean cereal (*Chenopodium quinoa*)
quintal	equivalent to one hundred pounds
supai	spirit of a mountain, rainbow, etc.
tarea	measurable labour task; i.e. to clean 10 m of an irrigation channel
tragu	sugar-cane alcohol; liquor
yanapero	a labourer of a hacienda who had access to pasture and firewood in compensation to labour given to the hacienda

Sources

1: Archivo Nacional de Historia, Quito, Protocolos 140 (1867–8), Notaria 4ª (Mariano Soria), pp. 371.
2: Carmen Hess, Fabian Montesdeoca, and Luis Toro. Encuestas de Extension en Zumbahua (1990). Código Profogan Z3–349, pp. 1–12.
3: Carmen Hess. 130 Questionarios (socio-economico-cultural)—inclusive 10 pruebas (1989/1990). Código Profogan Z3–205, pp. 1–130.
4: J. S. P. para el Subsecretario de Previsión Social, oficio no. 8921-D-ASC, 3 de Julio de 1967.
5: Archivo Nacional de Historia, Quito, Protocolos 495 (1877–78), Notaria 1ã (Francisco Valdés), pp. 367.
6: Testamento de Pantaleon Estupiñan de 1909. Notario Carlos Sandoval, Latacunga.
7: Marco Garzón, Jaime Llanos, Carmen Hess. 27 Questionnaires (zootechnical) 1989/90; (a random sample of 20% of Michacalan families). Código Profogan Z3–205/1–27.
8: Marco Garzón, Jaime Llanos. Botanical composition of Michacalan paramos. Código Profogan Z3–434, Q–2146/p.
9: Alejandro Guanotuña, Carmen Hess. Temperature and rainfall measurements in Michacala from November 1989 to October 1991. Código Profogan Z3–287.

References

Acosta-Solís, Misael (1984) *Los Paramos Andinos del Ecuador.* Quito, Publicaciones Científicas MAS.

Aguiló, Federico (1987) *El Hombre del Chimborazo*, Serie Mundo Andino, Quito, Ediciones Abya-Yala.

Alberti, Giorgio and Mayer; Enrique (eds.) (1974) *Reciprocidad e Intercambio en los Andes Peruanos*, Lima, Instituto de Estudios Peruanos.

Allen, Catherine J. (1988) *The Hold Life has: Coca and Cultural Identity in an Andean Community*, Washington, Smithsonian Institution Press.

Amin, Samir (1974) *Accumulation on a World Scale: A Critique of the Theory of Underdevelopment,* (trans. by Brian Pearce), New York, Monthly Review Press.

Anderson, E.N. (1987) 'Why is Humoral Medicine so Popular?' *Social Science and Medicine*, 25, pp. 331–7.

Aristide, Jean-Bertrand (1990) *In the Parish of the Poor: Writings from Haiti*, New York, Orbis Books.

Aronowitz, Stanley (1993) 'Paulo Freire's Radical Democratic Humanism', in Peter McLaren and Peter Leonard (eds.) *Paulo Freire: A Critical Encounter*, London and New York, Routledge, pp. 8–24.

Asad, Talal (ed.) (1973) *Anthropology and the Colonial Encounter*, Atlantic Highlands, NJ, Humanities Press.

Balladelli, Pier Paolo (1990) *Entre lo Magico y lo Natural: La Medicina Indígena, Testimonio de Pesillo* (with collaborator Miguel Colcha), Quito, Abya-Yala.

Banco Central del Ecuador (1989–1990) *Información Estadística Quincenal*, 12, Quito, BCE.

Barth, Frederik (ed.) (1969) *Ethnic Groups and Boundaries: The Social Organization of Culture Difference*, London, George Allen & Unwin.

Bastian, Joseph W. (1989) 'Differences between Kallawaya-Andean and Greek-European Humoral Theory,' *Social Science and Medicine*, 28, pp. 45–51.

Bastian, Joseph W. and Donahue, John M. (eds.) (1981) *Health in the Andes,* Special Publication of the American Anthropological Association, 12. Washington, AAA.

Bebbington, Anthony (1991) 'Indigenous Agricultural Knowledge Systems, Human Interests, and Critical Analysis: Reflections on Farmer Organization in Ecuador', *Agriculture and Human Values*, Winter/Spring, pp. 14–24.

– (1993) 'Sustainable Livelihood Development in the Andes', *Development Policy Review*, 11(1), pp. 5–30.

Bello, Walden, Kinley, David and Elinson, Elaine (1982) *Development Debacle: The World Bank in the Philippines*, San Francisco, Institute for Food and Development Policy.

Belote, James and Linda S. Belote (1984) 'Suffer the Little Children: Death, Autonomy, and Responsibility in a Changing 'Low Technology' Environment', *Human Values*, 9(4), pp. 35–48.

– (1985) 'Vertical Circulation in Southern Ecuador', *Circulation in Third World Countries*, R. Mansell Prothera and Murray Chapman (eds.) London, Routledge and Keagan Paul, pp. 160–177.

Bennett, John W. (1988) 'Anthropology and Development: The Ambiguous Engagement', in *Production and Autonomy: Anthropological Studies and Critiques of Development*, John W. Bennett and John R. Bowen (eds.), Monographs in Economic Anthropology 5, Lanham, University Press of America, pp. 1–29.

Bhatnagar, Bhuvan and Williams, Aubrey C. (eds.) (1992) *Participatory Development and the World Bank: Potential Directions for Change*, World Bank Discussion Papers 183, Washington, The World Bank.

Bodley, John H. (1982) *Victims of Progress*, Palo Alto, Mayfield.

Boster, James S. and Weller, Susan C. (1990) 'Cognitive and Contextual Variation in Hot-Cold Classification', *American Anthropologist*, 92(1), pp. 171–9.

Botero, Luis F. (compilador) (1991) *Compadres y Priostes: La Fiesta Andina como Espacio de Memoria y Resistencia Cultural*, Colección Antropologia Aplicada, 3, Quito, Abya-Yala.

Bourque, Susan C. and Warren, Kay Barbara (1981) *Women of the Andes: Patriarchy and Social Change in Two Peruvian Towns*, Ann Arbor, University of Michigan Press.

Braaten, Jane (1991) *Habermas's Critical Theory of Society*, Albany, State University of New York Press.

Brokensha, David, Warren, D.M. and Werner, Oswald (eds.) (1980) *Indigenous Knowledge Systems and Development*, Washington, University Press of America.

Brokensha, David and Riley, Bernard W. (1980) 'Mbeere Knowledge of their Vegetation and its Relevance for Development: A Case Study from Kenya', in *Indigenous Knowledge Systems and Development*, David Brokensha et al. (eds.), Washington, University Press of America, pp. 111–27.

Browman, David L. (1974) 'Pastoral Nomadism in the Andes', *Current Anthropology*, 15(2), pp. 188–96.

Brush, Stephen B. (1977) *Mountain, Field, and Family: The Economy and Human Ecology of an Andean Valley*, Philadelphia, University of Pennsylvania Press.

Brush, Stephen, Carney, Heath J. and Huamán, Zosimo (1981) 'Dynamics of Andean Potato Agriculture,' *Economic Botany*, 35, pp. 70–88.

Brush, Stephen B. and Turner, B.L., II (1987) The Nature of Farming Systems and Views of their Change, in *Comparative Farming Systems*. B.L. Turner, II, and Stephen B. Brush (eds.) New York, Guilford Press, pp. 11–48.

Campaña, Victor A. (1991) *Fiesta y Poder: La Celebración de Rey de Reyes en Riobamba*, Colección Antropologia Aplicada, 2, Quito, Abya-Yala.

Cañadas, Luis (1983) *El Mapa Bioclimático y Ecológico del Ecuador*, Quito, MAG-PRONAREG (includes map: 1:2 000 000).

Cardoso, Fernando E. and Falletto, Enzo (1979) *Dependency and Development in Latin America*, (trans.by Marjory Mattingly), Berkeley, University of California Press.

Carrera Colin, Juan (1981) 'Apuntes para una Investigación Etnohistórica de los Cacicazgos del Corregimineto de Latacunga, Siglos XVI-XVII', *Cultura*, 11, Quito, Banco Central del Ecuador, pp. 129–69.

CEDIG (1985) *Demografía en el Ecuador: Una bibliografía. Poblaciones de las Parroquias–Ecuador 1950–1982*, Documentos de Investigación, Serie Demográfica 1 y 2, Quito, Ecuador.

CEPAL (1990) *Transformación Productiva con Equidad. La Tarea Prioritaria de América Latina y el Caribe en los Años Noventa*, (Comisión Económica para América Latina), Naciones Unidas, Santiago de Chile,

Cernea, Michael M. (1991) 'Knowledge from Social Science for Development Policies and Projects', in *Putting People First: Sociological variables in rural development*, Michael M. Cernea (ed.) New York, Oxford University Press, pp. 1–42.

– (1991) *Putting People First: Sociological Variables in Rural Development*, New York, Oxford Press.

– (1992) *The Building Blocks of Participation: Testing Bottom-up Planning*, World Bank Discussion Paper 166, Washington, The World Bank.

Chambers, Robert (1983) *Rural Development: Putting the Last First*, London, Longman.

– (1991) 'Shortcut and Participatory Methods for Gaining Social Information for Projects', in *Putting People First: Sociological Variables in Rural Development*, Michael M. Cernea (ed.) (2nd ed.), New York, Oxford University Press and The World Bank, pp. 515–37.

– (1994a) 'Participatory Rural Appraisal (PRA): Analysis of Experience', *World Development*, 22(9), pp. 1253–68.

– (1994b) 'Participatory Rural Appraisal (PRA): Challenges, Potentials and Paradigm', *World Development*, 22(10), pp. 1437–54.

Chiriboga, Manuel, Landín, Renato and Borja, Jaime (1989) *Los Cimientos de una Nueva Sociedad: Campesinos, Cantones y Desarrollo*, Quito, MBS–IICA.

Classen, Constance (1993) *Inca Cosmology and the Human Body*, Salt Lake City, University of Utah Press.

Claverías Huerse, Ricardo (1990) *Cosmovisión y Planificación en las Comunidades Andinas*, Lima, Dugrafis.

Clifton, James A. (ed.) (1970) *Applied Anthropology: Readings in the Uses of the Science of Man*, Boston, Houghton–Mifflin.

Cochrane, Glynn (1979) *The Cultural Appraisal of Development Projects*, New York, Praeger.

CONADE Consejo Nacional de Desarrollo (1987) *Población y Cambios Sociales: Diagnóstico Sociodemográfico del Ecuador, 1950–1982*, Quito, Corporación Editora Nacional.

Cordero, Luis (1989) *Quichua Shimiyuc Panca—Diccionario Quichua*, Quito, Educación Bilingue Intercultural, Corporación Editora Nacional.

Córdoba, Marcelo et al. (1988) *Diagnóstico Comunicacional sobre la Situación de las Organizaciones Campesinas de Cotopaxi*, Quito, CIESPAL.

Corkill, David and Cubitt, David (1988) *Ecuador: Fragile Democracy*, London, Russell Press.

Crain, Mary M. (1991) 'Poetics and Politics in the Ecuadorean Andes: Women's Narratives of Death and Devil Possession', *American Ethnologist*, 18(1), pp. 67–89.

Croll, Elisabeth and Parkin, David (1992) Anthropology, the Environment and Development, in *Bush Base: Forest Farm: Culture, Environment and Development*, Elisabeth Croll and David Parkin (eds.) London, Routledge, pp. 3–10.

Crandon-Malamud, Libbet (1991) *From the Fat of our Souls: Social Change, Political Process and Medical Pluralism in Bolivia*, Berkeley, University of California Press.

Custred, Glynn (1974) 'Llameros y Comercio Interregional', in *Reciprocidad e Intercambio en los Andes Peruanos*, Giorgio Alberti and Enrique Mayer (eds.), Lima, IEP, pp. 252–89.

DeWalt, Kathleen M. and DeWalt, Billie R. (1989) 'Incorporating Nutrition into Agricultural Research. A Case Study from Southern Honduras', in *Making our Research Useful: Case Studies in the Utilization of Anthropological Knowledge*, John van Willigen et al. (eds.) Boulder, Westview, pp. 179–99.

Dietz, James L. and James, Dilmus D. (eds.) (1990) *Progress towards Development in Latin America: From Prebish to Technological Autonomy*, Boulder, Lynne Rienner.

Dirección General de Geologia y Minas (1978) *Mapa Geológico de la Parroquia de Zumbahua*, Quito, DGGM.

Dove, Michael R. (1988) Traditional Culture and Development in Contemporary Indonesia, in *The Real and Imagined Role of Culture in Development: case studies from Indonesia*, Michael R. Dove (ed.) Honolulu, University of Hawaii Press, pp. 1–37.

Dubly, A. (1990) *Los Poblados del Ecuador: Estudio Geográfico*, Quito, Corporación Editora Nacional.

Dyson-Hudson, Neville (1991) 'Pastoral Production Systems and Livestock Development Projects: An East African Perspective', in *Putting People First: Sociological Variables in Rural Development*, Michael M. Cernea (ed.) New York, Oxford University Press, pp. 219–56.

Eddy Elizabeth M. and Partridge, William L. (1987) 'The Development of Applied Anthropology in America', in *Applied Anthropology in America*, E.M. Eddy and W.L. Partridge (eds.) New York, Columbia University Press, pp. 3–55.

Eisenstadt, Samuel N. (1973) *Tradition, Change, and Modernity*, New York, Wiley.

Elisabetsky, Elaine (1986) 'New Directions in Ethnopharmacology', *Journal of Ethnobiology*, 6(1), pp. 121–8.

Ensminger, M.E. (1970) *Sheep and Wool Science*, Danville, Interstate Publishers.

Erler, Brigitte (1985) *Tödliche Hilfe: Bericht von meiner letzten Dienstreise in Sachen Entwicklungshilfe*, Freiburg, Dreisam Verlag.

Escobar, Arturo (1991) 'Anthropology and the Development Encounter: The Making and Marketing of Development Anthropology', *American Ethnologist*, 18(4), pp. 658–82.

Estrella, Eduardo (1977) *Medicina Aborigen: La Práctica Aborigen de la Sierra Ecuatoriana*, Quito, Editorial Epoca.

- (1982) 'Urcu-camashca o Violación del Cerro', *Umiña: Revista Informatica del Ministerio de Salud Pública*, 1(2), Quito, pp. 31–2.

Europe World Year Book (1992) *Europe World Year Book*, Vol. 1, London, Europe Publications, pp. 959–74.

Evans-Pritchard, E.E. (1976) *Witchcraft, Oracles, and Magic among the Azande*, (Abridged with an introduction by Eva Gillies), [Orig. 1937], Oxford, Clarendon.

Fairhead, James (1993) 'Representing Knowledge: The 'New Farmer' in Research Fashions', in *Practising Development: Social Science Perspectives*, Johan Pottier (ed.) London, Routledge, pp. 187–204.

Ferguson, James Gordon (1990) *The Anti-Politics Machine: Development, Depoliticization, and Bureaucratic Power in Lesotho*, Cambridge, Cambridge University Press.

Fernandéz, Maria (1992) 'The Social Organization of Production in Community-Based Agropastoralism in the Andes', in *Plants, Animals and People*, Constance M. McCorkle (ed.) Boulder, Westview Press, pp. 99–108.

Ferrara, Alessandro (1990) 'A Critique of Habermas's Dikursethik', *The Interpretation of Dialogue*, Tullio Maranhâo (ed.), Chicago, University of Chicago Press, pp. 303–37.

Figueroa, Dimas (1989) *Paulo Freire zur Einführung*, Hamburg, Edition SOAK.

Finnegan, Ruth and Horton, Robin (1973) 'Introduction', in *Modes of Thought: Essays on Thinking in Western and Non-Western Societies*, R. Finnegan and R. Horton (eds.), London, Faber & Faber, pp. 13–62.

Flannery, Kent, Joyce Marcus and Robert G. Reynolds (1989) *The Flocks of the Wamani: A Study of Llama Herders on the Punas of Ayacucho, Peru*, London, Academic Press.

Flavier, Juan M., de Jesus, Antonio and Navarro, Conrado S. (1995) 'The Regional Program for the Promotion of Indigenous Knowledge in Asia (REPPIKA)', in *The Cultural Dimension of Development: Indigenous Knowledge Systems*, D. Michael Warren, L.Jan Slikkerveer, David Brokensha (eds.) London, Intermediate Technology Publications, pp. 479–87.

Flores Ochoa, Jorge A. (1968) *Los Pastores de Paratía: Una Introducción a su Estudio*, Cuzco, Inkarí.

- (1977a) *Pastores de Alpacas de los Andes. Pastores de Puna*, Jorge A. Flores Ochoa (ed.), Lima, IEP, pp. 15–54.

- (1977b) Enqa, Enqaychu, Illa y Khuya Rumi, op.cit., pp. 210–38.

- (1979) 'Desarrollo de las culturas humanas en las altas montanas tropicales. (Estrategias adaptativas)', in *El Medio Ambiente Páramo*, M.L. Salgado-Labouriau (ed.) Mérida, CEA, pp. 225–34.

- (1988) Mitos y canciones ceremoniales en comunidades de puna, *Llamichos y Paqocheros*, Jorge A. Flores Ochoa (ed.), Cuzco, CEAC, pp. 237–54.

Foster, George M. (1965) 'Peasant Society and the Image of Limited Good', *American Anthropologist,* 67, pp. 293–315.

- (1969) *Applied Anthropology*, Boston, Little, Brown and Company.

- (1973) *Traditional Societies and Technological Change*, New York, University of California.

- (1976) 'Disease Etiologies in Non-Western Medical Systems', *American Anthropologist,* 78, pp. 773–82.

Foster, George M. and Anderson, Barbara Gallantin (1978) *Medical Anthropology*, New York, Wiley.

Frank, André G. (1967) *Capitalism and Underdevelopment in Latin America: Historical Studies of Chile and Brazil*, New York, Monthly Review Press.

Frank, Erwin H. (1991) 'Movimiento Indígena, Identidad Etnica y el Levantamiento', in *Indios: Una Reflexión sobre e Levantamiento Indígena de 1990*, Ileana Almeida et al., Quito, ILDIS, pp. 499–527.

- (1992a) 'Für und Wider die Fünfhundertjahrfeier: Das Beispiel Ekuador', *Peripherie*, No. 43/44, pp. 45–58.

- (1992b) 'Geschichte und Utopie: Die indianische Bewegung in Ekuador', in D. Dirmoser u.a. (Hrsg.), *Die Wilden und die Barbarei, Lateinamerika Analysen und Berichte*, Jahrbuch, No. 16, Münster, pp. 48–65.

Franquemont, Christine et al. (1990) *The Ethnobotany of Chinchero, an Andean Community in Southern Peru*, Botany 24, Chicago, Field Museum of Natural History.

Freire, Paulo (1984) *Pedagogy of the Oppressed*, (trans. by Myra Bergman Ramos), New York, Continuum Publishing.

Fuenzalida-Vollmar, F. (1971) 'Poder, Étnia y Estratificación Social en el Perú Rural', in *Perú Hoy*, José Matos Mar (ed.) México, Siglo XXI, pp. 8–85.

Galt, Anthony H. (1991) 'Magical Misfortune in Locorotondo', *American Ethnologist*, 18(4), pp. 735–49.

Gangotena, Francisco (1981) Peasant Social Articulation and Surplus Transference: an Ecuadorian Case, Ph.D. thesis, University of Florida.

Geertz, Clifford (1973a) 'Deep Play: Notes on the Balinese Cockfight', *The Interpretation of Cultures*, selected esays by C. Geertz, New York, Basic Books, pp. 412–53.

Giddens, Anthony (1987) *Social Theory and Modern Sociology*, Stanford, CA, Stanford University Press.

Gilles, Jere and Keith Jamtgaard (1982) 'Overgrazing in Pastoral Areas: The Commons Reconsidered', *Nomadic Peoples*, 10, pp. 1–10.

Godoy, Ricardo A. (1984) 'Ecological Degradation and Agricultural Intensification in the Andean Highlands', *Human Ecology*, 12(4), pp. 359–83

Golte, Jürgen (1980) *La Racionalidad de la Organización Andina*, Lima, IEP.

Gondard, Pierre (1986) 'Cambio Históricos en el Aprovechamiento del Medio Natural Ecuatoriano: Papel de la Demanda Social', *Cultura*, Revista del Banco Central, Quito, VIII(24), pp. 567–78.

Good, Byron (1994) *Medicine, Rationality and Experience: An Anthropological Perspective*, The 1990 Lewis Henry Morgan Lectures, Cambridge, Cambridge University Press.

Good, Byron J. and Mary-Jo D. (1982) 'Toward a Meaning-Centered Analysis of Popular Illness Categories: 'Fright Illness' and 'Heart Distress' in Iran', in *Cultural Conceptions of Mental Health and Therapy*, Anthony J. Marsella and Geoffrey M. White (eds.) Dordrecht, D. Reidel, pp. 141–66.

Goulet, Denis (1985) *The Cruel Choice: A New Concept in the Theory of Development*, Lanham, University Press of America.

Grillo, Ralph and Rew, Alan (eds.) (1985) *Social Anthropology and Development Policy*, London, Tavistock Publications.

Grindle, Merilee S. (1986) *State and Countryside: Development Policy and Agrarian Politics in Latin America*, Baltimore: The Johns Hopkins University Press.

Gudeman, Stephen (1971) 'The Compadrazgo as a Reflection of the Natural and Spiritual Person', *Proceedings of the Royal Anthropological Institute of Great Britain and Ireland*, pp. 45–71

Guerrero, Andrés (1991) *La Semántica de la Dominación: el Concertaje de Indios*, Quito, Ediciones Libri Mundi.

Guillet, David W. (1980) *Risk Management among Andean Peasants*, Andean Peasant Economics and Pastoralism Publication 1, Small Ruminants – CRSP, University of Missouri Columbia, pp. 13–44.

– (1984) 'Agro-Pastoral Land Use and The Tragedy of The Commons in the Central Andes', *Proceedings of the Southern Anthropological Society*, 17, pp. 12–23.

Habermas, Jürgen (1976) 'Was heißt Universalpragmatik?' In *Sprachpragmatik und Philosophie*, Karl-Otto Apel (Hrsg) Frankfurt/Main, Suhrkamp, pp. 174–272.

– (1979) 'What is Universal Pragmatics?' *Communication and the Evolution of Society*, (trans. by Thomas McCarthy), Boston, Beacon Press, pp. 1–68.

– (1981) *Technik und Wissenschaft als 'Ideologie'*, Frankfurt/Main, Suhrkamp.

– (1983) *Moralbewußtsein und kommunikatives Handeln*, Frankfurt/Main, Suhrkamp.

– (1984a) *The Theory of Communicative Action: Reason and the Rationalization of Society*, Vol. 1, (trans. by Thomas McCarthy), Boston, Beacon Press.

– (1984b) *Vorstudien und Ergänzungen zur Theorie des kommunikativen Handlens*, Frankfurt/Main, Suhrkamp.

Hahold, Andres (1988) 'El Sistema Cálido-Fresco en la Región Surandina del Peru', in *Conceptos y Tratamientos Populares de Algunas Enfermedades en Latinoamerica*, Axel Kroeger and Wilson Ruiz Cano (eds.) Cuzco, Centro de Medicina Andina, pp. 37–53.

Harriss, John (1982) 'General Introduction', *Rural Development: Theories of Peasant Economy and Agrarian Change*, J. Harriss (ed.) London, Hutchinson University Library, pp. 15–34.

Haswell, Margaret R. (1975) *The Nature of Poverty: A Case-History of the First Quarter–Century after World War II*, New York, St Martin's Press.

Herzfeld, Michael (1981) 'Meaning and Morality: A Semiotic Approach to Evil Eye Accusations in a Greek Village', *American Ethnologist*, 8(3), pp. 560–74.

Hess, Carmen G. (1990) 'Moving up—Moving down: Agropastoral Land-Use Patterns in the Ecuadorian Paramos', *Mountain Research and Development*, 10(4), pp. 333–42.

– (1992) *La Racionalidad de una Economia Agropecuaria: Una Contribución hacia el Desarrollo en los Páramos Ecuatorianos*, Quito, Proyecto de Fomento Ganadero, MAG-GTZ.

– (1994) 'Enfermedad y Ética en los Andes Ecuatorianos', *Hombre y Ambiente*, 29, Quito, Abya-Yala, pp. 47–89.

Hoben, Allan (1982) 'Anthropologists and Development', *Annual Review of Anthropology*, 11, pp. 349–75.

– (1984) Role of the Anthropologist in Development Work: An Overview, in *Training Manual in Development Anthropology*, William L. Partridge (ed.), Washington, AAA, pp. 9–17.

Holdridge, L.R. (1967) *Life Zone Ecology*, San José, Tropical Science Center.

Hollis, Martin and Lukes, Steven (eds.) (1982) *Rationality and Relativism*, Cambridge, MIT Press.

Horster, Detlef (1990) *Habermas zur Einführung*, Hamburg, Junius.

Horton, Robin (1970) 'African Traditional Thought and Western Science', in *Rationality*, Bryan R. Wilson (ed.) Oxford, Basil Blackwell, pp. 131–71.

– (1982) 'Tradition and Modernity Revisited', in *Rationality and Relativism*, Martin Hollis and Steven Lukes, (eds.), Cambridge, MA, MIT Press, pp. 201–60.

Horton, Robin and Finnegan, Ruth (eds.) (1973) *Modes of Thought: Essays on Thinking in Western and Non-Western Societies*, London, Faber & Faber.

Horowitz, Irving L. (1967) *The Rise and Fall of Project Camelot: Studies in the Relationship between Social Science and Practical Politics*, Cambridge, MIT Press.

Howes, Michael (1980) 'The Uses of Indigenous Technical Knowledge in Development', *Indigenous Knowledge Systems and Development*, David Brokensha, D.M. Warren and Oswald Werner (eds.) Lanham, University Press of America, pp. 335–51.

Hughes, Charles C. (1968) 'Ethnomedicine', in *International Encyclopedia of the Social Sciences*, Vol. 10, David L. Sills (ed.) pp. 87–93.

Hunt, Linda L. (1992) Living with Cancer in Oaxaca, Mexico: Patient and Physician Perspectives in Cultural Context, Ph.D. thesis Harvard University.

Inamura, Tetsuya (1981) 'Adaptación Ambiental de los Pastores Altoandinos en el Sur del Perú', in *Estudios Etnográficos del Perú Meridional*, Shozo Masuda (ed.) Tokyo, Universidad de Tokyo, pp. 33–64.

INEC (Instituto Nacional de Estadística y Censo) (1991) *V. Censo de Población y IV. de Vivienda 1990: Resultados Definitivos—Provincia de Cotopaxi*, Quito, INEC.

Isbell, Billie J. (1978) *To Defend Ourselves*, Austin, University of Texas Press.

James, Wendy (1973) 'The Anthropologist as Reluctant Imperialist', in *Anthropology & the Colonial Encounter*, Talal Asad (ed.) Atlantic Highlands, Humanities Press, pp. 41–69.

Johnson, Allen W. (1978) *Quantification in Cultural Anthropology: An Introduction to Research Design*, Stanford, Stanford University Press.

Johnston, B.F. and P. Kilby (1982) "Unimodal' and 'Bimodal' Strategies of Agrarian Change', in *Rural Development: Theories of Peasant Economy and Agrarian Change*, John Harriss (ed.) London, Hutchinson University Library, pp. 37–65.

Kahn, Joel S. (1985) 'Peasant Ideologies in the Third World', *Annual Review of Anthropology*, 14, pp. 49–75.

Kearney, Michael (1975) 'World View Theory and Study', *Annual Review of Anthropology*, 4, Palo Alto, pp. 247–70.

Klarén, Peter (1986) 'Introduction', in *Promise of Development: Theories of Change in Latin America*, Peter F. Klarén and Thomas J. Bossert (eds.) Boulder, Westview, pp. 3–35.

Kleinman, Arthur (1980) *Patients and Healers in the Context of Culture: An Exploration of the Borderland between Anthropology, Medicine, and Psychiatry*, Berkeley, University of California Press.

Knapp, Gregory (1988) *Ecología Cultural Prehispánica del Ecuador*, Biblioteca de Geografía Ecuatoriana 3, Quito, Banco Central del Ecuador.

Lewis, Oscar (1959) *Five Families: Mexican Case Studies in the Culture of Poverty*, New York, Basic Books.

Lipton, M. (1977) *Why Poor People Stay Poor: Urban Bias in World Development*, London, Temple Smith.

Logan, Michael (1977) 'Anthropological Research on the Hot-Cold Theory of Disease: Some Methodological Suggestions', *Medical Anthropology*, 1, pp. 87–112.

Long, Norman (1977) *An Introduction to the Sociology of Rural Development*, Boulder, Westview.

López Austin, Alfredo (1984) *Cuerpo Humano e Ideología: Las Concepciones de los antiguos Nahuas*, Vol. 2, México, UNAM.

MacCormack, Sabine (1991) *Religion in the Andes: Vision and Imagination in Early Colonial Peru*, Princeton, Princeton University Press.

MAG (Ministerio de Agricultura y Ganaderia) (1989) *Estimación de la Superficie Cosechada: Producción y Rendimiento del Ecuador*, Quito, Ministerio de Agricultura y Ganaderia.

Masefield, G. B. (1976) 'Anthropology and Agricultural Extension Work', in *What We Can Do For Each Other: An Interdisciplinary Approach to Development Anthropology*, Glynn Cochrane (ed.), Amsterdam, B.R. Grüner, pp. 29–42.

Masuda, Shozo, Shimada, Izumi and Morris, Craig (eds.) (1985) *Andean Ecology and Civilization: An Interdisciplinary Perspective on Andean Ecological Complementarity*, Tokyo, University of Tokyo Press.

Maybury-Lewis, David (1984) 'Conclusion: Living in Leviathan, Ethnic Groups and the State', in *The Prospects of Plural Society*, D. Maybury-Lewis (ed.), Proceedings of the American Ethnological Society, Washington, AES, pp. 220–31.

– (1988) 'A Special Sort of Pleading: Anthropology at the Service of Ethnic Groups', in *Tribal Peoples and Development Issues: A Global Overview*, John H. Bodley (ed.), Mountain View, Mayfield Publishing, pp. 375–90.

– (1989) 'The Quest for Harmony', in *The Attraction of Opposites: Thought and Society in a Dualistic Mode*, David Maybury-Lewis and Uri Almagor (eds.) Ann Arbor, University of Michigan Press, pp. 1–17.

– (1992) A New World Dilemma: The Indian Question in the Americas, (Talk delivered to the American Academy of Arts and Sciences, Cambridge.

Mayer, Enrique and Bolton, Ralph (eds.) (1980) *Parentesco y Matrimonio en los Andes*, Lima, PUCP.

McCarthy, Thomas (1991) *Ideals and Illusions, On Reconstruction and Deconstruction in Contemporary Critical Theory*, Cambridge, MIT Press.

McCorkle, Constance M. (1982) *Organizational Dialectics of Animal Management*, Small Ruminant Collaborative Research Support Program, Publication 5, Department of Rural Sociology, Columbia, University of Missouri.

– (1983) Meat and Potatoes: Animal Management and the Agropastoral Dialectic in an Indigenous Andean Community with Implication for Development, Ph.D. thesis Stanford University.

– (1986) 'An Introduction to Ethnoveterinary Research and Development', *Journal of Ethnobiology*, 6(1), pp. 129–49.

– (1989) 'Veterinary Anthropology in the Small Ruminant CRSP/Peru', in *The Social Sciences in International Agricultural Research: Lessons from the CRSPs*, Constance M. McCorkle (ed.) Boulder, Lynne Rienner, pp. 213–27.

– (1992) 'The Agropastoral Dialectic and the Organization of Labor in a Quechua Community', in *Plants, Animals and People*, Constance McCorkle (ed.), Boulder, Westview Press, pp. 77–97.

McKee, Lauris (1988) 'Tratamiento Etnomédico de las Enfermedades Diarréicas de los Niños en la Sierra del Ecuador', in *Nuevas Investigaciones Antropologicas Ecuatorianas*, Lauris McKee and Silvia Argüello (eds.) Quito, Abya-Yala, pp. 189–98.

McLaren, Peter and Leonard, Peter (eds.) (1993) *Paulo Freire: A Critical Encounter*, London and New York, Routledge.

Mendelson, E. Michael (1968) 'World View', *International Encyclopedia of Social Sciences*, Vol. 16, pp. 576–9.

Messer, Ellen (1981) 'Hot-Cold Classification: Theoretical and Practical Implication of a Mexican study', *Social Science and Medicine*, 15b, pp. 133–45.

Monasterio, Maximina (ed.) (1980) *Estudios Ecológicos en los Páramos Andinos*, Mérida, Ediciones de la Universidad de los Andes.

Moore, Barrington, Jr. (1967) *Social Origins of Dictatorship and Democracy: Lord and Peasant in the Making of the Modern World*, Boston, Beacon Press.

Muñoz-Bernand, Carmen (1986) *Enfermedad, Daño e Ideología. Antropología Médica de los Renacientes de Pindilig*, Quito, Ediciones Abya-Yala.

Murra, John (1972) 'El Control Vertical de un Máximo de Pisos Ecológicos en la Economía de las Sociedades Andinas', in *Visita de la Provincia de León de Huánuco en 1567*, John Murra (ed.) Huánuco, Universidad Nacional Hermilio Valdizán, pp. 429–76.

Naranjo, Marcelo (coordinador) (1986) *La Cultura Popular en el Ecuador*, Cotopaxi, Tomo II, Quito, CIDAP.

Nash, June (1993) *We Eat the Mines and the Mines Eat Us: Dependency and Exploitation in Bolivian Tin Mines*, New York, Columbia University Press.

Oberem, Udo (1967) 'Zur Geschichte des lateinamerikanischen Landarbeiters: Conciertos und Huasipungueros in Ecuador', *Anthropos*, 62, pp. 471–526.

– (1978) 'El Acceso a Recursos Naturales de Diferentes Ecologías en la Sierra Ecuatoriana (Siglos XVI)', *Actes du XLIIe Congres Internacional des Americanistes*, Vol. IV, Paris, pp. 51–64.

Orlove, Benjamin S. (1977) *Alpacas, Sheep and Men: The Wool Export Economy and Regional Society in Southern Peru*, New York, Academic Press.

– (1981a) 'The Andean Herding Complex: New Studies on the Traditional Herders of the High Andean Puna', *Nomadic Peoples*, 8, pp. 27–34.

– (1981b) 'Native Andean Pastoralists: Traditional Adaptations and Recent Changes', in *Contemporary Nomadic and Pastoral Peoples: Africa and Latin America*, Philip Carl Salzman (ed.) Studies in Third World Societies 17, Williamsburg, College of William and Mary, pp. 95–136.

Palmer, Davd Scott (ed.) (1992) *The Shining Path of Peru*. New York, St Martin's Press.

Parry, Martin, Knapp, Gregory and Cañadas, Luis (eds.) (1987) *The Effects of Climatic Variations on Agriculture in the Central Sierra of Ecuador*, Laxenburg, International Institute for Applied Systems Analysis.

Parsons, Elsie C. (1945) *Peguche: Canton of Otavalo, Province of Imbabura, Ecuador: A Study of Andean Indians*, Chicago, University of Chicago Press.

Partridge, William L. (ed.) (1984) *Training Manual in Development Anthropology*, A Special Publication of the American Anthropological Association and the Society for Applied Anthropology, 17, Washington.

Pathy, Jaganath (1987) *Anthropology of Development: Demystifications and Relevance*, Delhi, Gian Publishing.

Pérez T. Aquiles R. (1962) *Los Seudo-Pansaleos*, Quito, Taller Gráficos Nacionales.

Peters, Pauline (1993) 'Is 'Rational Choice' the Best Choice for Robert Bates? An Anthropologist's Reading of Bates' Work', *World Development*, 21(6), pp. 1063–76.

Popkin, Samuel L. (1979) *The Rational Peasant: The Political Economy of Rural Society in Vietnam*, Berkeley, University of California Press.

Pottier, Johan (1993) 'Introduction: Development in Practice: Assessing Social Science Perspectives', in *Practising Development: Social Science Perspectives*, Johan Pottier (ed.) London, Routledge, pp. 1–12.

Pretty, Jules N., Guijt, Irene, Scoones, Ian, and Thompson, John (1995) *A Trainer's Guide for Participatory Learning and Action*, London, IIED.

PROFOGAN (Proyecto de Fomento Ganadero) (1988) *Estadísticas Pecuarias del Ecuador: 1950–1987*, Quito, PROFOGAN, MAG–GTZ.

– (1990) *Plan de Referencia 1990–1993*. (Unpublished report for document), Quito, MAG-GTZ.

– (1991) *Situación de la Pequeña y Mediana Explotación Pecuaria en el Ecuador: Análisis y Perspectivas de Sistemas de Producción de Seis Zonas Agroecológicas*, Quito, PROFOGAN, MAG–GTZ.

Quintero, Maria and Cotacachi, Merced (1986) *Quiquinllatac Quichua Shimita Yachacupai. Aprenda Usted Mismo el Quichua*, 7 volumenes, Quito, Instituto Nacional de Capacitación Campesina, Abya–Yala.

Ramón V., Galo (1987) *La Resistencia Andina: Cayambe 1500–1800*, Quito, CAAP.

– (1990) 'El Ecuador en el Espacio Andino. Idea, Proceso y Utopía', *Allpanchis*, xxii, no. 35/6.

Redclift, Michael (1987) *Sustainable Development: Exploring the Contradictions*, London, Routledge.

Reiter, Rayna. R. (1975) 'Men and Women in the South of France: Public and Private Domains', in *Toward and Anthropology of Women*, Rayna R. Reiter (ed.) New York, Monthly Review Press, pp. 252–82.

Richards, Paul (1985) *Indigenous Agricultural Revolution: Ecology and Food Production in Western Africa*, London, Hutchinson.

Robertson, Alexander F. (1984) *People and the State: An Anthropology of Planned Development*, Cambridge, Cambridge University Press.

Rosaldo, Michelle Z. (1980) *Knowledge and Passion: Ilongot Notions of Self and Social Life*, Cambridge, Cambridge University Press.

Rostow, W.W. (1964) *The Stages of Economic Growth: A Noncommunist Manifesto*, London, Cambridge University Press.

Rubel, Arthur J., O'Nell, Carl W. and Collado, Rolando (1985) 'The Folk Illness Called Susto', in *The Culture-Bound Syndromes: Folk Illnesses of Psychiatric and Anthropological Interest*, Ronald C. Simons and Charles Hughes (eds.) Boston, Reidel Publishing, pp. 333–45.

Sachs, Wolfgang (ed.) (1992) *The Development Dictionary: A Guide to Knowledge as Power*, London, Zed Books.

Salmen, Lawrence (1987) *Listen to the People: Participant–Observer Evaluation of Development Projects*, World Bank Publication, New York, Oxford University Press.

Salomon, Frank (1983) 'Shamanism and Politics in Late-Colonial Ecuador', *American Ethnologist*, 10(3), pp. 413–28.

Sarmiento, G. (1986) 'Ecological Features of Climate in High Tropical Mountains', in *High Altitude Tropical Biogeography*, François Vuilleumier and Maximina Monasterio (eds.) New York, Oxford University Press, pp. 11–45.

Scheper-Hughes, Nancy (1992) *Death Without Weeping: The Violence of Everyday Life in Brazil*, Berkeley, University of California Press.

Schueler, Elizabeth (1989) 'Culture in Development or Development in Culture', *A Journal of Development Studies*, Fletcher School, Medford, pp. 26–30.

Scott, James C. (1985) *Weapons of the Weak: Everyday Forms of Peasant Resistance*, New Haven, Yale University Press.

– (1990) *Domination and the Arts of Resistance: Hidden Transcripts*, New Haven, Yale University Press.

Servaes, Jan, Jacobson, Thomas L. and White, Shirley A. (eds.) (1996) *Participatory Communication for Social Change*, New Delhi et al., Sage Publications.

Sheahan, John (1987) *Pattern of Development in Latin America: Poverty, Repression and Economic Strategy*, Princeton, Princeton University Press.

Sillitoe, Paul (1993) 'The Development of Anthropology', MAN, 28 (3), p. 597f.

Slikkerveer, L. Jan and Dechering, Wim H.J.C. (1995) 'LEAD: The Leiden Ethnosystems and Development Programme', in *The Cultural Dimension of Development: Indigenous*

Knowledge Systems, D.M. Warren, L.J. Slikkerveer, D. Brokensha (eds.) London, Intermediate Technology Publications, pp. 435–40.

Sola, José (1992) 'Ecología de Monataña y Prácticas Terapeúticas Campesinas', in *Medicina Andina: Situaciones y Respuestas*, varios autores, Quito, CAAP, pp. 85–121.

Stark, Louisa R. and Pieter C. Muysken (1977) *Diccionario Español-Quichua, Quichua-Español*, Publicación 1, Guayaquil, Quito, Museos del Banco Central del Ecuador.

Starn, Orin (1991) 'Missing the Revolution: Anthropologists and the War in Peru', *Cultural Anthropology*, 6(1), pp. 63–91.

Strathern, Marilyn (1981) 'Self-interest and the Social Good: Some Implications of Hagen Gender Imagery', in *Sexual Meanings: The Cultural Construction of Gender and Sexuality*, Sherry B. Ortner and Harriet Whitehead (eds.) Cambridge, Cambridge University Press, pp. 166–91.

Stutzman, Ronald (1981) '*El Mestizaje*: An All-Inclusive Ideology of Exclusion', in *Cultural Transformations and Ethnicity in Modern Ecuador*, Norman E. Whitten, Jr. (ed.) Urbana, University of Illinois Press, pp. 45–94.

Swantz, Marja-Liisa (1985) 'The Contribution of Anthropology to Development Work', *Anthropological Contributions to Planned Change and Development*, Harald O. Skar (ed.), Gothenburg Studies in Social Anthropology 8, Göteburg, Acta Universitatis Gothoburgensis, pp. 18–32.

Tambiah, Stanley J. (1990) *Magic, Science, Religion, and the Scope of Rationality*, The Lewis Henry Morgan Lectures 1981, Cambridge, Cambridge University Press.

Theis, Joachim and Heather M. Grady (1991) *Participatory Rapid Appraisal for Community Development, A Training Manual based on Experiences in the Middle East and North Africa*, London, Save the Children and IIED.

Thomas, R. Brooke (1977) 'Adaptación Humana y Ecologia de la Puna', in *Pastores de Puna: Uywamichiq Punarunakuna*, Jorge A. Flores Ochoa (ed.) Lima, IEP pp. 87–112.

Thrupp, Lori A. (1989) 'Legitimizing Local Knowledge: Scientized Packages or Empowerment for Third World People', in *Indigenous Knowledge Systems: Implications for Agriculture and International Development*, D.M. Warren, L.J. Slikkerveer and S.O. Titilola (eds.) Studies in Technology and Social Change, No.11, Ames, Iowa State University, pp. 138–53.

Tomoeda, Hiroyasu (1985) 'The Llama is my Chacra: Metaphor of Andean Pastoralists', in *Andean Ecology and Civilization: An Interdisciplinary Perspective on Andean Ecological Complementarity*, Shozo Masuda, Izumi Shimada and Craig Morris (eds.) Tokyo, University of Tokyo Press, pp. 277–99.

– (1988) 'La Llama es mi Chacra', in *Llamichos y Paqocheros*, Jorge A. Flores Ochoa (ed.) Cuzco, CEAC, pp. 225–36.

Torres Fernandez de Cordova, Glauco (1982) *Diccionario Kichua-Castellano: Yurakshimi-Runashimi*, Tomo I, Cuenca, Ecuador, Casa de la Cultura del Azuay.

Tousignant, Michael (1988) 'La Teoria Quichua de las Emociones: Un Ejemplo de la Provincia de Bolivar', in *Nuevas Investigaciones Antropológicas Ecuatorianas*, Lauris McKee and Silvia Argüello (eds.), Quito, Abya–Yala, pp. 189–98.

Turner, B.L. and Stephen B. Brush (eds.) (1987) *Comparative Farming Systems*, New York, The Guilford Press.

Turton, David (1988) 'Anthropology and Development', in *Perspectives on Development: Cross-disciplinary Themes in Development Studies*, P.F. Leeson and M.M. Minogue (eds.) Manchester, Manchester University Press, pp. 126–59.

UNDP (United Nations Development Programme) (1993) *Human Development Report, 1993*, New York, Oxford University Press.

Uphoff, Norman (1991) 'Fitting Projects to People', in *Putting People First: Sociological Variables in Rural Development*, Michael M. Cernea (ed.) New York, Oxford Press, pp. 467–511.

Van den Berg, Hans (1990) *La tierra no da así nomás: Los Ritos Agrícolas en la Religión de los Aymara-Cristianos*, La Paz, Bolivia, HISPOL.

Vogt, Evon Z. (1976) *Tortillas for the Gods: A Symbolic Analysis of Zinacanteco Rituals*, Cambridge, Harvard University Press.

- (1990) 'Cruces Indias y Bastones de Mando en Mesoamérica', in *De Palabra y Obra en el Nuevo Mundo*, Vol. II, Manuel Gutiérrez Estévez, Miguel Leon-Portilla, Gary H. Gossen, and J. Jorge Klor de Alva (eds.) Encuentros interétnicos, Madrid, Siglo XXI de España, pp. 249–94.

Walker, Jim (1981) 'The End of Dialogue: Paulo Freire on Politics and Education', *Literacy & Revolution: The Pedagogy of Paulo Freire*, Robert Mackie (ed.) New York, Continuum, pp. 120–50.

Wallerstein, Immanuel (1974) *The Modern World-System. Capitalist Agriculture and the Origins of the European World-Economy in the Sixteenth Century*, Vol. I, New York, Academic Press.

Warren, D. Michael, Slikkerveer, L. Jan, and Brokensha, David (eds.) (1995) *The Cultural Dimension of Development: Indigenous Knowledge Systems*, London, Intermediate Technology Publications.

Warren, D. Michael and McKiernan, Gerard (1995) 'CIKARD: A Global Approach to Documenting Indigenous Knowledge for Development', in *The Cultural Dimension of Development: Indigenous Knowledge Systems*, D. Michael Warren, L. Jan Slikkerveer and David Brokensha (eds.) London, Intermediate Technology Publications, pp. 426–34.

Weber, Max (1978) *Economy and Society: An Outline of Interpretive Sociology*, Vol. I, Günther Roth and Claus Wittich (eds.) Berkeley, University of California Press.

Webster, Steven S. (1973) 'Native Pastoralism in the South Andes', *Ethnology*, 12(2), pp. 115–33.

Weismantel, Mary (1988) *Food, Gender and Poverty in the Ecuadorian Andes*. Philadelphia, University of Pensylvania Press.

West, Terry (1988) 'Rebaños Familiares – Propietarios Individuales: Ritual Ganadero y Herencia Entre los Aymara de Bolivia', in *Llamichos y Paqocheros*, Jorge A. Flores Ochoa (ed.) Cuzco, CEAC, pp. 191–201.

White, Alan (1982) *Hierbas del Ecuador*, Quito, Ediciones Libri Mundi.

White, Stuart and Maldonado, Fausto (1991) 'The Use and Conservation of Natural Resources in the Andes of Southern Ecuador', *Mountain Research and Development*, 11(1), pp. 37–55.

Whitten, Norman E., Jr. (1985) *Sicuanga Runa: The Other Side of Development in Amazonian Ecuador*, Urbana and Chicago, University of Illinois Press.

WHO (World Health Organization) (1992) *World Health Statistics Annual* Geneva, World Health Organization.

Wilson, Bryan R. (ed.) (1970) *Rationality*, Oxford, Basil Blackwell.

Winch, Peter (1958) *The Idea of a Social Science*, London, Routledge.

- (1970) 'Understanding a Primitive Society', in *Rationality*, Bryan R. Wilson (ed.) Oxford, Basil Blackwell, pp. 78–111.

Wing, Elizabeth (1986) 'Domestication of Andean Mammals', in *High Altitude Tropical Biogeography*, François Vuilleumier and Maximina Monasterio (eds.) New York, Oxford University Press, pp. 246–64.

Winterhalder, B., Larsen, R. and Thomas, R. Brooke (1974) 'Dung as an Essential Resource in a Highland Peruvian Community', *Human Ecology*, 2(2), pp. 80–104.

Worsley, Peter (1984) *The Three Worlds: Culture and World Development*, Chicago, University of Chicago Press.

Wright, Susan and Nelson, Nici (1995) 'Participatory Research and Participant Observation: two incompatible approaches', in *Power and Participatory Development: Theory and Practice*, Nici Nelson and Susan Wright (eds.) London, Intermediate Technology Publications, pp. 43–59.

Yamamoto, Norio (1985) 'The Ecological Complementarity of Agro-Pastoralism: Some Comments', in *Andean Ecology and Civilization*, Shozo Masuda, Izumi Shimada and Craig Morris (eds.) Tokyo, University of Tokyo Press, pp. 85–99.

Zúñiga, Neptali (1980) *Significación de Latacunga en la Historia del Ecuador y América*, Tomo I, Latacunga, Talleres Editoriales.